THE
ILLUSTRATED
ANGLER

THE ILLUSTRATED ANGLER

The Classic Text of
Trevor Housby
and
Original Paintings by
Charles Jardine

BLANDFORD

A BLANDFORD BOOK
First published in the UK 1996 by Blandford
A Cassell Imprint
Wellington House
125 Strand
London
WC2R 0BB

Distributed in the United States by Sterling Publishing Co., Inc.
387 Park Avenue South, New York, NY 10016–8810

British Library Cataloguing-in-Publication Data
A Catalogue record for this book is available from the British Library.
ISBN 0–7137–2189–8

Printed and bound in Hong Kong by Dah Hua

CONTENTS

FOREWORD

ANGLING IN THE 1990s is now a truly global sport. Buy an around-the-world air ticket and you could fish for bonefish in the Bahamas, king salmon in Alaska, yellow-fin tuna off Hawaii, black marlin off the Great Barrier Reef, brown trout in Tasmania, sailfish off Malindi, wahoo off Maderia – finishing with sea trout in the west of Ireland. What a mouth-watering prospect!

Despite the commercial pressure on our migratory game fish, particularly from Far Eastern fishing boats, anglers have been able to stay one step ahead of the game. But this international sport may not last for ever. The world's demand for fish has never been higher and, despite shrinking stocks, larger commercial boats are still being constructed.

Today's international angler needs to know when and where the fish are running. His tackle must be of the highest technical merit. His boat driven by engines powerful enough to travel more than 100 miles in a day, and run back to port before any storm.

Trevor Housby, the author of this book and the father of international game fishing in the UK, had no such concerns when he started on his illustrious angling career. Even 20 years ago, wild game fish stocks were in a much more healthy state than they are today.

Trevor could roam the world catching big fish at will. He was the pioneer, breaking new ground for European anglers after big fish, particularly in the waters off Portugal, Madeira, the Canary Islands and the Azores. In addition to catching sharks of monumental size, Trevor predicted that the semi-tropical waters of the Eastern Atlantic were home at certain times of year to blue marlin of world record weight. What a tragedy that he is no longer with us to witness his prediction come true, as the top marlin skippers from around the world move their boats to the Portuguese and Spanish islands. Blue marlin of more than 1000lb have now also been caught off the mainland Algarve coastline.

To the stillwater trout angler, Trevor will always be remembered as the man who gave us the Dog Nobbler – that totally outrageous, but incredibly successful, fishing fly with the lump of lead at its head that makes it so fatally attractive to rainbows. Trevor devised the controversial pattern after fishing with American bass jigs. British trout had seen nothing like it, and fell head over heels for it.

Living in Hampshire, Trevor had access to the best small stillwater trout fisheries in the country. And the crystal clear waters of lakes like Avington, Damerham and Rockbourne gave him the opportunity to experiment with his new fly's action. However, his favourite trout water of all was Leominstead, a peaceful haven hidden away among the rhododendrons and beech trees of the New Forest near his Lymington home. It was here that he would relax over a glass or two with its colourful owner Leo Jarmal. Sadly, neither angler is still with us.

I was in my teens when I first met Trevor Housby in the angling department of Gamages, the traditional Holborn department store that sold everything from model trains to mens' suits. Editor of a monthly Fleet Street fishing magazine at the time, this friendly giant of a man used to hold regular court at lunchtime with the customers and staff.

Over the passing years, I came to know Trevor well. We shared boats together off Ireland and the Needles and caught trout at waters like Lakedown and Damerham. Yet only once did I catch more than him. We were fishing for cod in a Bergen fiord, and bites were hard to come by. The hospitality was excellent, with a continual supply of fresh prawn sandwiches. It was only when I started baiting the hooks with the prawns that I started to catch in earnest. Trevor never did learn my secret.

A day with Trevor was about much more than catching fish. His humour and anecdotes were inimitable, although many of his death-defying tales of adventure took some swallowing. A former backing guitarist of Tommy Steele, and regular player at the Soho beatnik haunt The 2-Is coffee bar, Trevor took his 12-string with him around the world to charm and entertain. We shall not see his like again.

I hope that you enjoy reading Trevor's stories of battles with giant game fish from around the world, brought alive by the creative genius of angling artist Charles Jardine. Trevor's writing will no doubt continue to inspire anglers for many years to come. So share his dreams and adventures in the following pages . . .

Chris Dawn
Editor *Trout Fisherman*

INTRODUCTION
by Charles Jardine

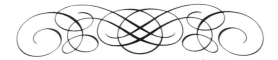

I WRITE THIS introduction half a world away from normal routine, in a hotel room in Georgetown, Great Exuma, in that tropical island paradise – the Bahamas. I have just returned from the vast and pearly flats, flanked by turquoise and sapphire, which are the home of one of the world's premier sporting quarry: bonefish, otherwise known as the wily fox of the flats. Trevor would have appreciated this world – it was his, too. He would also have relished the heart-stopping, reel-churning, knuckle-biting flight of a 'bone' fleeing across the crystal waters in a headlong dash for the ultramarine horizon.

This book is unashamedly about such places, fish and dreams. It was a world in which Trevor toured and which he constantly brought to life through word and film during his colourful time with us, now sadly over. Trevor died during the production of this book, but he would not like me to be over-sentimental. Nevertheless, let me start at the beginning. . . .

The sun was dancing across Damerham's depths when I spied a roundish, bearded, bear-like man patrolling Vicarage Moor, the furthest lake. We were introduced by a mutual friend, Bill Sibbons, and this was the start of many angling adventures together. Fishing with Trevor was always an 'adventure', through the years spent both at Damerham, the Broadlands carrier on the Test and, latterly, Bossington Lake. Here one day, Trevor and I, having caught a good few rainbows and brook trout, decided to deviate a little and pursue (hotly, I should add), with our fly rods, a raft of carp swimming near an island. If I remember correctly, we both caught one on a White Muddler under, shall we say, 'dubious' circumstances – we 'chummed' them with bread! As I said, fishing with Trevor was always an adventure.

Most anglers knew him through either his deep-sea, big game sagas or 'dog nobbling', but these were only parts of a multifaceted fishing career. In this book you will see the full breadth of Trevor's fishing world – it simply knew no bounds. Indeed, I can recall his books on pike and eel fishing when I was just in my teens.

Whatever Trevor fished for he generally learnt something about it – most importantly, how to deceive it and catch it. My problem has been how to depict these aspects, and many people have been 'press-ganged' into helping me, from my cousin Dr David Molyneux, now Head of the Liverpool School of Tropical Medicine, who knows much about tropical waters, through David, to Dr Vaughan Southgate at the British Museum of Natural History who authenticated the fish, if needed. I also relied on references in one form or another and, the most vital ingredients, personal knowledge and experience. This was my excuse to my family for ventures to Canada, the USA and the Bahamas.

This book also gave me a unique opportunity to try different media. I felt that new challenges were needed, and new methods and materials. It has been a voyage of discovery, every bit as much as that of Trevor's fishing world. You will see within these pages a huge array of styles and techniques. Hopefully, each will have portrayed something special about the fish and the world that they inhabit. This is always the artist's aim – atmosphere. For the record, I used Raphael and Winsor & Newton sable brushes (00–¼ in flats), Raphael watercolour paints, Winsor & Newton oils, Liquitex acrylics and Daler Board watercolour surfaces and canvas.

The book has taken an enormous length of time to reach fruition and my deepest thanks go to Peter Burton, who has steered it through uncharted, choppy, troubled water on more than a few occasions. I hope he feels, as I do, that it has been worth it!

I look back on the long journey now and, as with all such occasions, there is regret and emotion. However, the main feeling is joy, not only that the book is finished, but also that I worked with Trevor on a combined project. Writers, artists and musicians are lucky in that when we depart we are able to leave something of ourselves behind – no matter how small – for other generations. Trevor was more fortunate than most because he left behind a great deal that people will read and cherish. I feel glad I was able to work on this, Trevor's last book, and I hope I have done him justice.

Adieu, old friend, and to you, the reader, *'bon voyage'*. I hope you enjoy the journey through exotic waters, curious fish and dream fishing.

1
RAINBOW TROUT

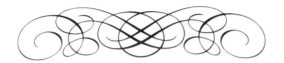

ONCE CONFINED TO the western slopes of the Pacific coast from Mexico to Alaska, the rainbow trout (*Salmo gairdneri*) has since been cultured and transplanted to almost every country in the world. This is a hardy, tough species, and one that is more adaptable to change than many other trout species. In its sea-run, or steelhead, form it attains great weights and, even in freshwater, fish weighing up to 40lb have been caught and recorded.

Farmed extensively throughout Europe and the USA, the rainbow has come to serve two main purposes. It was originally nurtured as a table fish – a cheap way of providing good fish for a receptive public – and most fish farms still produce the rainbow simply for the food market. Other farms, however, raise the trout solely for re-stocking major fishing waters. This trend started in the USA, where hundreds of tons of immature rainbows were distributed annually.

In Europe things moved more slowly; then in the late 1960s put-and-take trout fisheries began to spring up. Some reservoirs had long been stocked with a mixture of brown and rainbow trout, and the newly created fisheries came midway between the rivers and the reservoirs. The demand for put-and-take trout fishing was so great that within a decade hundreds of established and newly dug waters catered for a new breed of trout fishermen. This demand led to an increase in trout farms, which, in turn, led to increased growth rates in farm-bred stock fish. No longer were anglers satisfied with two brace of fish weighing 5–6lb together. What they wanted were individual fish of similar, or preferably greater, weights. A rainbow that was once classed as a glass-case specimen now became a run-of-the-mill fish. First the 10lb barrier was crossed, yet still the anglers wanted more. And this is where the Avington superstrain came into being. The late Sam Holland, who at that time owned Avington trout farm and lakes, came up with a theory. He reckoned that, by using the larger than average eggs from a very large hen rainbow, it should be possible to produce fry that were larger and faster growing than those produced from the eggs of a hen fish of the normal size, and it would seem that his calculations were correct. Today's put-and-take trout angler has the opportunity to put a fly over trout of 20lb and more, and 30lb is the next barrier to cross, a barrier that will vanish in the next few seasons. Producing fish of this size is a long, costly exercise, but the rewards are high and growing higher, as the demand for monster trout accelerates.

I have never understood this obsession with monster rainbow, greatly preferring to catch a 2½- to 3½-pounder in peak condition. The monsters are no more than old brood fish in their last year of life, and their only claim to fame is their huge size. They fight in a wallowing fashion, showing none of the vigour of a young rainbow. The smaller fish have style, and every once in a while you hook an outstanding fighting fish, the sort of trout you remember through a lifetime of fishing. Every angler has one such fish. Mine came from a small lake, fed directly from the River Test and actually looking more like a stretch of river than a still water. Rich in insect life, this fishery produces excellent catches although it does not give up its trout easily.

On the day I caught my rainbow the clouds were gathering and there was more than a hint of rain the air. There was a strange absence of trout on the surface, which left me the option of working a shrimp or a nymph across the bottom. I chose to fish over an area where a hidden sand bar reaches halfway to the surface. The fly was a golden shrimp imitation. Over the years I have found this version of the mating shrimp deadly, and I hoped that on this day it would be its usual productive self. To get the shrimp down I chose to use a sink-tip line, and my plan was to get the shrimp down fast and to work it in slow hops across the sand bar. On the third cast I felt a trout tweak at the fly. It was not a real take, more of an inquiry from an inquisitive fish, but even so it meant that I was using the right shrimp pattern. For a dozen more casts nothing further happened. Then, just as I was thinking that I should move along, the shrimp was taken with a bang. There was nothing tentative about this take – no tweaks, no warnings, just a solid pull from a fish that ripped the fly line down to the backing. For the next ten minutes the trout fought harder than any still-water rainbow I have ever seen. Its reactions to the dragging pull of the fly line were savage, and no sooner did I get most of the line back, than the fish tore off in a new direction. There was no way that I could dominate the early stages of the fight, but finally, of course, the trout began to weaken. By this time I had assumed that it was a big fish in prime condition, a perfect rainbow weighing 8–9lb. Its runs were too fast and too long for even a big brown trout, and so, with size in mind, I made sure the net was in working order and began to bring the exhausted fish to the bank. I had that rainbow in the net and on the bank before I realized it was not a big fish at all but at most weighed no more than 4½lb. Fin-perfect, with a broad band of magenta along its flank, it was in prime condition. It took less than a couple of seconds to extract the shrimp, which was lodged in the corner of its mouth, and put the fish back in the lake. I simply did not have the heart to kill it. A fish that fights so long and hard deserves its freedom, and I was happy to see it go. Fighting stock fish are few and far between and, when one does get caught, the angler concerned rarely forgets it. I have caught rainbow trout throughout the world, but this fish was outstanding.

Sea-run steelhead rainbows are quite different from the average stock fish. Life in the open ocean obviously suits them. They eat well, battle against the tidal system and grow fast and strong, ready for their return to the parent river. Steelhead are found in abundance from northern California to the Pacific northwest, and Washington State's Olympic Peninsula, where a series of rivers sweeps down through the mighty rainforest valleys and on to the sea, is an excellent spot. Nearly all those fishing rivers have Native American names – the Hoh, the Queets, the Quillayute and the Quinault, to name just a few – and the Native Americans have the rights to net salmon and steelhead in the river mouths. The rod-angler get his chance further upstream, as the fish head for the spawning grounds of the Olympic National Park. This is wild country, where wet days are the norm and the fish run big.

Traditionally, the American steelhead angler is not a purist. True, in the 1920s and 1930s Zane Grey fished with fly for incoming steelhead, but the average angler still prefers to use a fish bait or an artificial lure for steelhead. There is, however, a growing interest in fly-fishing for these splendid fish. The favoured local method is to drift-fish the river, using a cluster of salmon eggs wrapped in red mesh. Steelhead dearly love to feed on salmon eggs, and this bait will produce fish when all else fails. A good substitute is a few grains of tinned sweetcorn, which work presumably because they are egg-shaped and have the slightly salty flavour of the real thing. One thing is sure – the fish love them. In fact, anything that resembles a salmon egg can be used to good effect, and some anglers even use spinners tipped with a Day-Glo synthetic that is formed to look like eggs. Equally popular, however, is the true plug or spoon bait. The favourite plug has always been the banana-shaped, flatfish-style lure, which has the action of a crippled fish. Steelhead love an easy meal, and the gait of this unlikely plug seems to bring out the killer instinct in them.

Most of the river systems along the Pacific coast carry snow water or excess spare water, and for this reason the currents are strong, which is probably why true fly-fishing was seldom used. In the early years, silk fly lines just did not get the fly down to fish level. The breakthrough came in the early 1950s, when a line manufacturer introduced a fly line that incorporated a metal element. Soon after, the fast-sinking Wet Cel lines appeared, making it possible to cast to a marked fish and know that the fly would get down to it. Since those early days, lines have changed greatly, and most line manufacturers now produce lines with specific sinking speeds. Some lines have a lead core; others have powdered lead incorporated in the

PVC coating. Some lines, like the Hi-Di or Deep Water Express, will instantly cut through all but the worse of river currents. To complement the fast-sinking lines, new flies and lures have been tied – the Optic, for example, with its painted brass ball head, flies with heavy copper or lead wire underbodies, and the Dog Nobbler from Britain, which is a lead-headed lure with a long, flexible, marabou tail that is taking trout on an unprecedented scale.

Interestingly, although rainbow trout are heavily stocked in European rivers that flow into the sea, not one authenticated steelhead has been recorded in these waters. It is possible that the farm-reared fish have no specific roots and do not feel the urge to run a particular river. Anglers must hope that the steelhead will become a feature of the European fishing scene. The rainbow is a commonly stocked species, and it may be that, as more go truly wild, they will become established. The tragic loss of once-prolific Atlantic salmon stocks has left plenty of scope for sea-run rainbows to take over.

2
BROWN TROUT AND SEA TROUT

THE EUROPEAN BROWN TROUT (*Salmo trutta*) is a distinctive yet sadly diminishing species. Pollution, over-fishing, acid rain and the inroads made by commercial fish farms have taken their toll of the natural stocks in many lakes and rivers. In its sea-run state the brown trout – sea trout – is also an endangered species. Commercial netting and global warming have exacted a terrible penalty on this fish, and once prolific sea trout rivers are now virtually dry and, in many cases, denuded of returning sea trout and the resident wild 'brownies'.

As a child, I lived and fished in the west of England, and the streams around my home were full of plump, little, red-spotted brown trout. When I was young I was far from being a purist. My rod was a willow stick, matched to an equal length of line, but neither rod nor line was important. What counted was the hook and so-called catgut trace. Only one brand was reckoned to be good enough for trout fishing, and even now I can remember spending my hard-earned pennies on those hooks. The brand I sought was Lucky Strike, and the hooks were manufactured by the long-defunct company of Alcock in Redditch, Worcestershire. The fact that Alcock also made beautiful rods, reels and angling accessories never occurred to me – it was the Lucky Strike hooks that were important in my young life. Looking back, I can recall many a catch of bright little four-to-the-pound brown trout from those tiny dancing streams. I used worm as the bait, but I know it was those special hooks that caught me those prized fish.

Those days, long since gone, started me on a life devoted to all aspects of angling. I know the islands of the world, and I know the ways of great marlin and tuna, and the joys of stalking bonefish across the coral flats. All that has been mine because of those first hungry, often suicidal, wild brown trout. Since those halcyon days I have caught brown and sea trout in many places, and I have seen the rise of king rainbow trout as a stock species. Fish farmers have the knowledge to produce 30lb rainbow trout, and like most anglers I have flirted with these stew-fed monsters. But I have finally come to the conclusion that I would rather catch one lovely, wild brown trout than a host of pot-bellied, regenerated brood fish. Rainbow trout are fine in their own environment, but in Britain they do not breed freely, if at all, in the wild. The lovely wild brown trout, on the other hand, still struggles to breed successfully in its home waters.

If it is true wild brown you want, you must go to wild places. The tiny streams of southern England, Wales, the Yorkshire Dales or the islands of Scotland are the places to head for. Here, you will find the true stronghold of the wild brown trout. The much-vaunted chalk streams of the south may lay claim to exclusive brown trout fishing, but while those fat 4-pounders of the Kennet, Test and Itchen may look like the real thing, they are charlatans. These farm-bred fish, raised from much interbred Loch Lever stock, have little in common with the wild brown trout. Handsomely spotted these mighty trout may be, but they do not carry those tiny red spots that are the mark of the real thing. Catch a true brown, and no matter what its size, it is infinitely superior to its interbred cousin. Interestingly, the tiny, stunted 'brownies' of some long-neglected stream will grow if they are given right conditions. I have fished clear Cornish quarry pools that yield fat 4lb-plus browns. These fish could have come only from nearby streams, and presumably in time of flood the tiny trout were washed into the food-rich quarry waters to grow fat on the flies, nymphs and water snails that scarcely exist in the rather acid waters of their native streams.

Many of Scotland's lovely lochs are full of small brown trout. Other, deeper lochs may contain fewer but larger trout, however, and these great loch fish seldom fall to fly tackle. Instead, they are caught by a handful of hardy anglers who fish season after rugged season for just a small number of large fish. The ferox trout, as they are called, are big fish that have grown fat on a diet of small trout, char and various white fish, and such fish rarely rise to fly. They are vicious and voracious fish, and a large trolled spoon brings the best

results. This ferox fishing is a rough and rugged sport, which suits only a few hardy individualists, for it is a sport of bleak, cold weather, with the waters of some lonely lochs running high and dangerous. The rewards are few but fabulous. When a great, spotted ferox brown trout hits a glistening spoon, the rod top pulls hard down and the battle begins. These loch fish run big. A 10-pounder is a good fish but nothing out of the ordinary, for ferox can achieve weights exceeding 20lb. A fish of 15–17lb is a prize – a glistening monster – to be netted, photographed, carefully weighed and usually returned.

For most anglers, ferox are just something to be read about. Life is too short for the average angler to commit the time required to this endless trolling, with one eye on the rods, the other on the echo-sounder. For those who prefer to take brown trout on fly, the places to head for are the lochs of Orkney or the brown trout loughs of Ireland. In Ireland the cream of the fishing comes when the mayflies hatch, to live and die in a few short hours. This is the dapping time, when the bankside bushes are scoured to fill bait tins with newly hatched mayflies. These are fished live, on long dapping rods and blow lines made of the finest floss. The richly spotted fish of the Irish loughs throw caution to wind at mayfly hatch. Obsessed by the living fly, they often rise in abandon to glut themselves on the natural insect. Many anglers travel to Ireland during dapping time – and who can blame them? A basket of Corris brown trout is a prize that no chalk-stream angler can hope to match.

The lochs of Orkney are different. They are wilder than the great waters of Ireland and are steeped in the history of the great Viking years. Many a longship came to Orkney, and the men of the winged helmet and battle axe have left their presence on many of the Orcadian lochs. Lochs Harray, Swannay, Stennels and many more have this feel of ancient people, and in keeping with their past the trout-fishing methods on these lochs have remained traditional. The standard technique is to fish two to a boat with a loch gillie as a guide. The rods are long, and the cast carries three traditional flies, one of which is almost certainly a version of the local ke-he, a fly developed on Loch Harray in the 1930s. Said to represent a long-extinct type of bee, the ke-he is still a good fish catcher, often raising trout when all else fails. These Harray fish are not big. The odd monster has been taken over the years, but such fish are rare. Two brace of 1½-pounders is a good catch, one to lift the heart of any worthwhile trout man.

Swannay Loch produces larger fish, but the loch is an acquired taste. It is a dark, peaty pit of a loch, which broods in silence on even the brightest of days and gives up its trout with reluctance. If Swannay likes you, you will catch trout; if it does not like you, you may fish for weeks without raising a single one. There is a bitterness about Swannay that few men can conquer; it has a wildness of times long gone and of silent Norsemen buried within a stone's throw of its peaty shores. Once fished, Swannay is never forgotten, however, and one fish from its depths is a prize for any discerning angler.

When brown trout run to sea they grow sleek and silver on the rich feeding grounds beyond the river mouths, where young herring, sand eel, prawns and scuttling crabs provide the sea trout with growth-boosting calories. What always amazes me about sea trout is the range of rivers that produce them. Short, fast, rocky rivers produce mostly small fish of 1–3lb. In the West Country these bright silver fish are called peal, elsewhere they are known as sewin, or finnock. They are scrappy little night-feeders, which strike at fly, spinner or natural bait. The big sea trout, those fish weighing 10–20lb, come from the slower rivers. The Sussex Ouse, which is almost canal-like in its placidness, produces huge sea trout, and the sluggish rivers of the New Forest produce equally large fish. I saw a specimen of 17lb 9oz taken from the slow-moving Avon, a forest stream no more than 8 miles in total length. The Dorset Stour and, to a lesser extent, the Hampshire Avon produce huge sea trout. Then there are the sea trout runs of western Scotland and southern Ireland. In the west of Ireland they call them white trout and, when the white trout run, work stops and everyone goes fishing, for setting a sizeable sea trout cavorting across the water's surface creates its own special memories.

All this is good reason why the native wild brown trout should be preserved and protected. Without these game little survivors we would have no ferox, no sea trout and few memories for future angling generations to pass on. Without our true wilds' fish, trout fishing will eventually be nothing more than memories. Long may those existing stocks continue to thrive.

3
GREAT LAKE TROUT

CALLED LAKE TROUT, this fish (*Salvelinus namaycush*) is actually a char, albeit a very large one. Among the Salmonidae, the 'laker' is second in terms of weight only to the mighty and almost unknown taiman of Siberia and the great Chinook salmon. The record for a rod-caught lake trout stands at 65lb, a monster caught from the depths of Canada's Great Bear Lake, but even this huge fish pales into insignificance against the commercial record for this species – a fish of a staggering 102lb taken in set gill nets staked out in Lake Athabasca, Saskatchewan.

Essentially a cold-water species, lake trout prefer water temperatures of around 50°F. Temperatures above 60°F are far too warm for them to flourish. They are lovers of deep water and will occasionally descend to depths of over 400ft. Once the subject of intense commercial fishing techniques, the trout of the Great Lakes also suffered badly when lampreys invaded their waters some years ago but, fortunately, stocks are now well on the way to recovery. Lake trout were once confined entirely to the cold-water lakes and river systems of North America, but they have been transplanted to a handful of lakes in the west as well. Their diet is extremely varied but consists largely of insects, plankton and various types of small fish, and they are particularly fond of smelt and white fish. Lake trout spawn in the late fall, shedding eggs indiscriminately in the marginal shallows. Their colour varies from one water to another. The commonest colour is dark grey, with an irregular pattern of light spots, but in some waters they can be green, brown or almost black. As might be expected lake trout have several local names – Mackinaw trout in Alaska and togue in Maine, for example. In most good waters lake trout of 6–10lb are commonplace, but many weighing 20–30lb are taken during most seasons.

White Lake Rainbow ~ Oncorhynchus mykiss ~
Kamloops. NB far more silver than usual:
almost like Graham overwinter fish
very few spots and exceptionally big fins.

Mark bottom
flanked by weeds (pondweed)
Mark = Carina encrusted weeds; like a Coral Reef.
V white - Slash - against weed

Anglers are greatly divided in their opinion of the fighting ability of the lake trout. Some anglers claim that even a large laker puts up absolutely no resistance when hooked, but it would seem that the fighting capabilities of a hooked laker depend entirely on how far down the fish has been caught. A laker taken on a very deep-running down-rigger lure will seem to come up like a log, obviously a victim of changing water pressures. However, hook the same fish just under the surface and it may fight like a tiger. One thing a laker will not do is jump. All its fight is from the surface downwards.

In the northern river systems, lake trout feed mostly on insects, which makes them an ideal target for the fly-rodder, and because they are seldom selective feeders, they will hit just about any nymph or lure pattern. Hooked on a standard fly outfit, the lake trout is capable of fighting its weight at any time. Quite a few fish will be lost when the leader snags on the trout's numerous, large, sharp teeth.

Fly-casting for lake trout is not widely practised, however, and most American anglers prefer to spin or troll for their fish. Spin-fishing can be great fun, but it really works only when the surface and sub-surface temperatures are 50°F or less. At these times the lakers will feed within casting range of the shoreline. When the temperatures rise much above 50°F, the fish drop back into the cold depths.

I was once fortunate enough to arrive at the Lakes roughly ten days after an ice melt. My guide assured me that this was optimum time to take lake trout in the top water, but it has been my experience that guides are inclined to tell the angler just what he wants to hear, and so I naturally assumed that once again I was being offered some meaningless fishing lore. I could not have been more wrong, and my guide was spot-on with his calculations. At my second cast a good fish hit my frantically darting spinner and shot off like a rocket. My guide just nodded his head in satisfaction. I offered a mental apology and got on with the business of trying to control what was obviously a big, powerful laker. Finally the battle was over, and a great, sleek, grey-green trout slid alongside the boat. I am always amazed at how long in the body the lake trout is compared with others of the trout tribe, and this one looked all head and lean body. The gaudy, copper and white spoon dangled from its jaw. My guide carefully reached down to take the hooks out, and looking down at the laker's teeth I could see why he was cautious. The fish's jaws seemed to be studded with teeth that would not have looked out of place in the mouth of a barracuda. The instant the hooks came free, the fish was gone, a flick of its forked tail driving it instantly out of sight. At an estimate it weighed 12–14lb, which is a good fish for the comparatively shallow water. During the course of that short day I must have caught a dozen more and, although the first was the largest, the others were all good fish. They all fell to the same spoon, and by the end of the session much of its paint had been scraped away.

Compared with casting along the shore lines, deep-water trolling is a dull pastime. To get the lure down to fish level, the line has to be clipped to the lead ball of a down-rigger set-up. The second a trout hits the deep-running lure, the line snaps out of the clip. The only advantage is that the angler is in direct contact with the fish, and there is no lead on the line to deaden the pull of the trout – not that these deep-water fish pull that hard. This down-rigger fishing is by far the most popular way of catching lake trout, probably because it normally produces lots of big fish during the effective trolling season. Lake trout are not shoal fish in the accepted sense of the word, but rising water temperatures send a host of individuals scurrying into the depths, and these fish tend to congregate at points where the temperature suits their needs. Once such a cold-water 'hot-spot' is discovered, the trolling boats move in for the killing, and it is not unusual to see four boats hooked up at the same time. The trout seldom seem to sense the danger in a fast-moving lure, possibly because they are competing with their immediate neighbours and simply take whatever comes their way.

In the early years of this century people hand-lining for lake trout used a highly polished metal dinner plate as an attractor lure. This plate was attached to the heavy hand-line at a point several yards in front of the actual spinner, and the turbulence and flash generated by the plate attracted cruising trout from considerable distances.

For enterprising anglers who have the stamina, ice-fishing offers a great deal of scope. Basically, this is a form of deep jigging. The angler cuts a hole through the ice, sets up a wind shelter and seat, then settles back to work a jig-type lure on a short rod. It must be remembered that many North Americans fish to fill the deep freezer rather than for sport, and ice-fishing is both fun and an effective way of taking fish in quantity. Often the frozen lakes are covered with anglers, barbecues are set up, and a festive attitude prevails.

The truly large 'trophy' lake trout, weighing upwards of 40lb, are normally very old fish, possibly forty or fifty years old. One fish actually reached the age of sixty-plus years. Because of its comparative slow rate of growth, anglers now realize the need to conserve their stocks, and some fishing lodges stipulate that only 'trophy' fish can be killed. If its not big enough for the taxidermist, it goes back alive. Let us hope that this policy will ensure that the lake trout will continue to thrive in its ice-bound kingdom.

4
CHAR AND AMERICAN BROOK TROUT

IN BRITAIN AND Europe the char (*Salvelinus alpinus*) exists in only a few of the deeper, colder waters, and what was once a migratory species has become happily landlocked, appearing to have little trouble in spawning successfully. In Arctic seas, however, these fish still spend much of their time in saltwater, returning to their parent rivers only to breed. In most European lakes char seldom reach a weight of more than 1½lb, and many are smaller than this. There are one or two exceptions to this rule, and in recent years several specimens weighing over 5lb have been caught. All these fish have come from water almost 500ft deep.

In the Lake District of England char are comparatively abundant, and on Coniston Water there has long been a unique method of taking these fish commercially. Like trout, char feed to some extent on small fish, and on Coniston the traditional technique is to fish from a slowly moving rowing boat, using a pair of heavy poles as primitive outriggers. A long line and heavy lead are used on each pole to take a line of special spinners down almost to the lake's bed. Traditionally, the spinners were fashioned by hand from gold coins, gold being the colour that char find most attractive. A bell is attached to the tip of each outrigger, and when this rings to indicate that a fish has been hooked, the line of spinners is raised by a secondary handline attached to the actual fishing line. Crude as this technique may sound, it is an effective way of catching deep-water char, which would be beyond the reach of ordinary angling techniques. The real gold, hand-forged lures have long since vanished into museums and private collections, and today's char fishermen use gold anodized lures instead. The average angler has little opportunity to fly-fish for char, because the fish are usually too deep for fly-fishing or even for general spinning techniques. The alternative is to bait-fish using worm baits.

During early March Coniston Water char move up out of the deeps to feed at the comparatively shallow depth of 100–130ft, and I was once invited to take part in an expedition to the lake to try for the elusive char and, if successful, to take photographs for a magazine. The Lake District in March is cold, very cold, and even though we had a warm bed and a hot meal at night, the thought of arriving at the lakeside at dawn and sitting there until dusk was hardly appealing. The first morning found us slithering around ice-bound lakeside roads through woods turned white with hoar-frost. Our objective was a sort of headland jutting out into the lake, because local information stated that this was one of the places where char congregated. The tackle was basic – a long casting rod, a fixed-spool reel and enough lead and line to reach the bottom – and the bait was a bright red worm. Conditions were said to be near perfect. Perfect for the char, maybe, but not for the angler. By mid-morning none of us had had a bite, and the watery sunlight of early morning had vanished. Instead, intermittent snow squalls and leaden skies were rapidly lowering the morale of the party. Then, just as our spirits were at their lowest, the fish hit the baits. Everyone got a bite, and everyone netted a char. These were not just fish – they were living jewels, bright bars of colour that had to be seen to be believed. Now that the fish were on the feed, the atrocious weather was forgotten. We had come 300 miles to catch char, and now we were inundated with fish. Thoughts of cancelling the three-day trip were forgotten, for with fish like this, the cold and misery were irrelevant. That day we caught over forty of the world's loveliest freshwater fish. With a few deep-hooked exceptions, all were returned after they had been photographed. The next morning we were back. Expectations ran high, but the fish were gone, and by midday it was obvious that the snow clouds would not blow over. As we left lovely Coniston Water the roads were already thickly covered, and later, back in the south, we heard that the Lake District roads had become impassable and would remain so for several weeks. No matter, we had caught our fish, the photographs were excellent and the few fish we had kept were delicious. The only other place I ever caught char was from a lake in central Norway. The fish, which were not big, would feed on sunken flies and tiny spinners.

The American brook trout (*Salvelinus fontinalis*) is the original brook trout of North America, a fish that has inspired thousands of writers to produce millions of words on a fish that is still considered by many to be the ultimate North American fish. Good to catch, good to eat and beautiful to look at, the brook trout is, in fact, a char rather than a true trout, but little matter, for in the cold-water streams of North America it rises freely to the fly. Many a noted American angler began his career casting to 'brookies'. Sadly, however, brook trout stocks have long been on the wane. Many Americans blame the demise of brook trout in some areas on the widespread stocking of the European brown trout, and there can be no doubt that the introduction of alien species may have played a

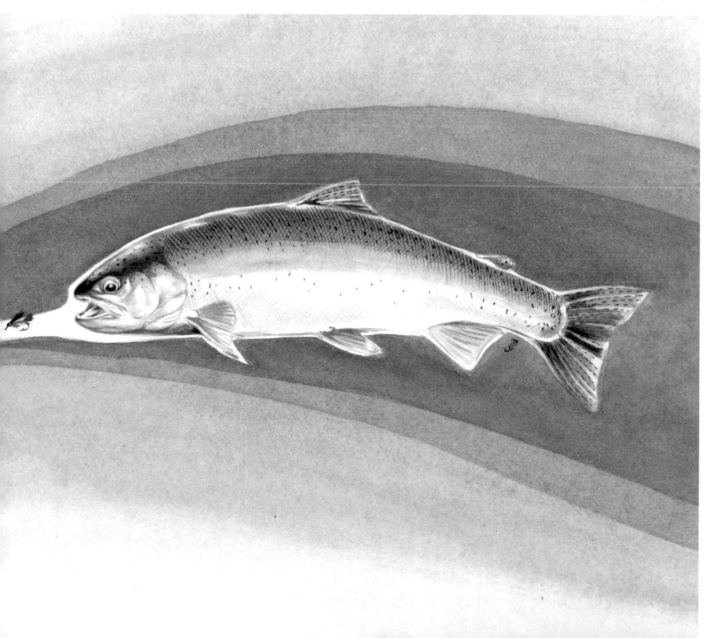

part in a fall in fish stocks. It is more likely, however, that deforestation has done the major damage. When trees fall, water temperatures rise, and in its native state the 'brookie' is very much a cold-water species. Brook trout are easily farmed, and this has led to many restocking programmes, although sadly few of them have met with any great measure of success.

In European waters this is far from the case. Since the late 1980s brook trout have been successfully raised on both British and European fish farms. The new put-and-take fisheries have in particular benefited from being stocked with these highly attractive fish. When they are introduced alongside stock brown and rainbow trout, the brook trout seem to thrive. They also have an intrinsic novelty value, and an angler who is used to catching good-sized brown and rainbow trout will enthuse over one smallish brook. The colours, the white-edged pelvic fins and the huge jaws of the adult males make for a striking fish.

I caught my first brook trout in England well over twenty years ago, and I have been a devoted fan of the species ever since. Those first brookies came from a private lake, which had remained unfished for several seasons and which was fed by underground springs, so the water remained icy even on hot days. This constant chill obviously appealed to the resident brook trout population, which had been stocked as fingerlings and grown on accordingly. The time of fishing was mid-spring, the leaves were just out on the willow trees, and primroses were growing in profusion on the untrodden banks. As is the case on all new waters, it was hard to know where to start. The water was deep and clear, and there were no obvious weed banks. I was, I must admit, unconvinced that the lake held trout of any sort but, having travelled a considerable distance to fish, I set up my tackle more in hope than expectation. Then, with everything correctly assembled, it was time to choose a fly. When you are familiar with a water and its fish, it is a simple task to predict the pattern or colour of the day. On a new, unfished water it is not so easy. In those days I was a nymph fanatic, and I decided on a nondescript grey-brown pattern, with which I had had much success on the chalk streams. False-casting to gain distance, I dropped the nymph well out from the bank, waited to let the nymph sink a little and then began the familiar figure-of-eight retrieve. I had gained scarcely a yard of line when something latched on to the fly. From the onset I was not quite sure what I had hooked. The fish did not fight in the dashing style of a rainbow, nor in the sullen, circling manner of a brown trout. Instead, its tail was going like an outboard motor, while its head was kept hard down towards the lake bed. At this time I knew nothing of the fighting technique of the brook trout, and I assumed that I had hooked a small pike or, possibly, a perch. My thought that it was a pike seemed to be confirmed when I caught a flash of a green, dappled side. Then my pike turned magically into a magnificent 2½lb brook trout. That first brookie was so wondrous and fascinating that I could hardly tear my eyes from it. The smooth, almost scaleless skin, the tiny magenta spots and the overall greeny gold colour were, without question, something very new. That day I caught four good brook trout and a solitary bright-striped rainbow trout. The broad colour band of the rainbow would normally have delighted me, but next to the subtle colours of the brookies it looked almost garish. Since that day I have caught a great many brook trout, but I never get used to them. Every one I see is a delight, and long may this remain so.

In the past decade or two fish farmers have developed an interesting hybrid by crossing a male brook trout with a female brown trout. These hybrids, known as tiger trout, are a vividly coloured version of the true brook trout. Highly aggressive tiger trout make good stock fish, although they are difficult to raise in quantity. The largest tiger trout I have seen weighed in at 7lb, but most are 2–4lb. Like the brook trout, the tiger can be colour conscious. Flies incorporating fluorescent yellow or orange will induce takes when drabber patterns fail to excite the fish. The brook trout may be an alien species to European waters, but as far as I am concerned it is a most welcome introduction.

5
GRAYLING
The Lady of the Stream

ANGLERS ARE EITHER for grayling or they are 'agin 'em', and this leaves the poor old grayling (*Thymallus thymallus*) in a sort of piscatorial limbo. Those who like them are usually free-thinkers and good anglers. They respect the grayling for its ice age ancestry, its beauty, its fighting ability and its subtle coloration. For such fishermen the grayling is a fish of clear rivers, the well-aerated shallows of high summer and the deep, gravel-bottomed pools of ice-bound winter. The opposing faction are usually fishermen who seldom catch much, the self-confessed 'experts', whose lack of trout can be conveniently blamed on the ever-active grayling. 'Too many darn grayling in the water' is a complaint that many river-keepers hear almost daily. They may hear it, but they do not necessarily believe that the grayling does much, if any, harm. There is usually a special place in the river system, a stretch of water that produces good-sized grayling, but that also normally produces even bigger trout. Grayling are sensitive to water quality. They will not tolerate pollution or a fall-off in the population of aquatic insects and, if the grayling shoals start to thin out, it is a poor keeper or riparian owner who does not take notice and look for the reasons. Some of the finest grayling are found on the chalk streams of England. They were an introduced species, but that was a long time ago, and the grayling stocks of today have been established for so long that they probably have more right to be in the river than the increasingly stocked rainbow trout.

However you look at it, the grayling is a survivor. The species has taken everything that man and nature can hand out, yet has continued to thrive against abnormal odds. From the angler's point of view, grayling have an immense advantage over trout. During the summer months they can be caught on dry fly and nymph and then, when winter sets in and the trout season closes, they can be fished with float and worm. This makes the grayling a fish for all seasons and a wonderful species for any angler. Fortunately, it is really only the English who regard the grayling as a form of aquatic vermin. In Canada, Arctic Norway, Austria and many other countries, grayling are welcomed and preserved as they should be.

One of the best times to go grayling fishing is on a bright but cold, crisp day in December or early January – the sort of day when the air is thin and clear, and the hoar-frost stays on the ground until late morning. Cold-weather grayling have a liking for deep pools on the bends of a river, where they sometimes gather in large shoals, waiting for whatever food the river brings them. Such fish will take a wet fly or leaded shrimp, but that is not the real way to fish for them, for fly tackle is a thing of the spring, summer and early autumn. After the first frost your fly tackle should be cleaned and relegated to the rod rack and fishing room. No, the way to fish for winter grayling is with the traditional float and worm. Izaak Walton fished this way

with pole and fixed line. Today's anglers use ultra-modern trotting rods and free lines, fished from a traditional centre-pin reel. There are many patterns of centre-pin available, but for grayling the finest must be a pre-war Alcock's Aerial. Never easily obtainable, the Aerial was a beautifully machined precision instrument, which turned freely to the slight drag of a float in running water. The modern fixed-spool reel may be perfect for spinning but, when it comes to working a river's conflicting currents, the old-fashioned centre-pin cannot be equalled.

Over the seasons I have spent many thousands of hours working a brightly tipped float through countless pools on many rivers. Probably my happiest days were spent on the tiny River Dever, a chalk stream, which ultimately runs into the Test at Barton Stacey, Hampshire, and which is the sort of water where seasonal trout fishing is expensive. The winter grayling fishing, on the other hand, costs nothing more than a bottle to the keeper: whisky is the pass-key to many wild and wonderful pieces of water. Like the Test, the Dever is a rich water, and even on the coldest days there will be a spasmodic fly hatch. I have seen trout and grayling rising in a snow storm, proof that, as Roderick Haigh Brown wrote, 'a river never sleeps'. Grayling fishing is essentially a roving sport, and often during the course of a winter's day I cover several miles of river bank, taking a fish here or a fish there. Sometimes, however, a shoal of big grayling will take up temporary residence in one pool and, when this happens, I may spend much of the day on just the one pool. I remember one such day on the junction pool where the River Dever flows into the Test. This particular pool is long and narrow, giving the angler a good 30 yards of near-perfect trotting water. I always liked to fish on the junction pool, and on this day I decided to start there – perhaps it was one of those angling premonitions that all anglers get from time to time. As always, I set up my tackle at the thatched fishing hut, and as always I took time to admire the painted wooden salmon on the walls. Then, with rod in hand and my coffee flask, bait tin and spare tackle in a shoulder bag, I walked down to the pool. As usual, I had my landing net hanging from a D-ring on my jacket. Later it was in so much demand that it stayed open and extended until an owl-haunted twilight drove me from the river.

I knew the pool over its entire length and had pre-set my float accordingly. Taking up a position at the head of the pool, I baited my hook with a worm. Grayling love worms but not just any worm. What they like is a true, bright, lively red worm. Although they will take marsh worm or the foul-smelling brandling, it is the true red worm that really holds their attention. As always, it was a pleasure to flick the floats out into the water's flow and to feel the exquisitely balanced centre-pin start to turn with the pull of the river. Grayling like to swim and feed just above the river bed, and I had set my tackle so that the bait hung an inch or so above the gravel. Halfway down the pool, the float bobbed twice and shot across the current. 'Darn, a trout,' I thought, and it did, indeed, turn out to be a rakish, out-of-season brown that would have weighed a good 3lb in August but now scaled no more than 2lb. Once played out, the fish was unhooked and released into the water. I hoped it would be the only trout in the pool.

For ten minutes I worked the float constantly through the length of the swim without a sign of fish interest. Obviously, either the splashing of the trout had scared the grayling or there were simply none in the pool to begin with. Then, as the float reached the tail end of the swim, it was dragged under, almost as if the hook had got caught on a weed strand. This dragging style of bite is something of a trade mark with grayling, and I reacted instantly. Setting the small hook with a long sideways sweep of the rod, I hooked grayling number one, which used its large dorsal fin to hold across the current. I knew it was a good size from the power of the fish, but I did not realize that it would weigh close to 3lb, a monster of a grayling, even by chalk-stream standards. From that first fish onwards, the pool produced grayling after grayling. None was quite as large as that first fish, but a fair number were over 2lb and a few under 1lb. I lost track of how many grayling I took that bright but bitterly cold day, but my estimate is between sixty and eighty fish. Occasionally the pool would die for ten or fifteen minutes, and then it would spring back to life, almost as though there was an endless shoal of fish entering the pool from the River Test. Not all grayling days are productive as this, of course. I was lucky and had picked the right pool on exactly the right day.

I once spent the best part of a warm June afternoon in pursuit of just one large grayling. Again I was having a day's fishing on the Dever for brown trout. The weather was fine, the weed growth lush and the fly hatch abundant. I had one fish of around 4lb early, and was looking for a larger trout to complete my limit. I had worked nearly a mile of river and located plenty of good, but not outstanding fish. Four-pounders are not uncommon on this river and, if I am honest, I must admit that I was after one of the occasional 5lb fish.

Then, at a point where a tiny side stream enters the main river beneath a trailing willow branch, I saw it. At first sight I couldn't believe its size – not a trout, but an immense grayling with a huge dorsal fin. I had caught grayling to 3lb, but those looked tiny compared with this vast fish. At that second, trout fishing was dismissed from my mind. Who wanted to catch trout when there was a chance of a record grayling? The fish was not rising, but it was feeding, and, through nearly 2ft of clear water, I watched it regularly move sideways from its position, each movement coinciding with an opening and closing of the mouth. The fish was clearly nymphing, but the question was, what type of nymph was it on? Try as I might I could not see the tiny insect or its colour. My only hope was to go through my nymph box until I found a pattern it would move to. I must have tried a dozen nymphs before the fish looked at a tiny copper nymph. He did not take it, but he definitely looked it over. I waited for five minutes and made another cast. The same thing happened. Obviously, I had to make this grayling an offer it could not refuse, so I decided to be bold. Off came the tiny version of the copper nymph, to be replaced by a similar pattern, but tied on a much larger hook. I dropped the nymph ahead of the stationary fish, and as it came downstream the grayling moved forwards to intercept it. I saw the mouth open and close, and I struck as the nymph vanished. Instantly the fish tore off upstream and my light leader parted. I shall never know how big that grayling really was. It was without question well above the record size, but how much above it was impossible to say. And what does it matter anyway? I had induced the fish to food, I had hooked it and then lost it, but I wasn't going to cry over it.

6
ATLANTIC SALMON

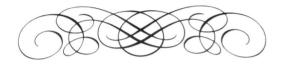

OVER THE PAST decade the plight of the Atlantic salmon (*Salar salar*) has become the subject of international concern. Once prolific salmon rivers, famous for their runs of prime fish, now produce little for anglers spending their money each season. The days of good fishing at reasonable cost are over, and salmon anglers now have to travel to Labrador, to the Kola Peninsula in Russia or to the top rivers of Norway. This is costly fishing, which only the privileged few can afford.

Less than ten years ago things were different. Anglers could fish for a reasonable seasonal fee or they could join association waters and still manage a few good fish each year. Since then, salmon prices have risen and the oceanic holding grounds have been plundered. The few fish that have escaped the big trawlers have mostly succumbed to legal or, more often, illegal inshore netsmen. To compound the felony, the seas have also been deluded of the creatures on which salmon naturally feed. Prawns, herrings and sand eel are caught in increasing quantity, and this has led to the few salmon that have escaped the netsman running later and later. Out-of-season fish are of little use to the rod-and-line angler.

The saving of the Atlantic salmon must now be a matter of economic pressure. When fish stocks are reduced to a point at which they are no longer a viable proposition, then, and only then, will the pressure of fishing be reduced. Unfortunately, by that time it may be too late to save the Atlantic salmon as we know it, and this is the cost of putting too great a value on the price of wild-salmon flesh. True, the extensively ranched salmon may in time become a market filler, but at present the demand is not for pellet-fed salmon. Restaurants, gourmets and hoteliers want wild fish.

It was not always thus. There was a time when salmon steaks, cutlets and wafer-thin slices of smoked salmon were a delicacy that only the favoured few could enjoy. Increased commercial catches then made salmon widely available, and it gained popularity with the public. Before this upsurge in the sales of salmon flesh, rivers teemed with fish. Individual beats produced hundreds of salmon each season, and during this heady period a rod on a good river could be had at reasonable cost and the angler could rely on catching fish. It is clear that the salmon runs of most rivers had been in slow decline for many, many years, however. It is only necessary to read the books and fish records of the 1920s and 1930s to realize that catch rates used to be very high. Rod catches did not deplete the stocks of mature fish, however. The balance of nature became tipped against the salmon's survival only when the fish-buying public started to eat the flesh regularly.

I can remember fishing the River Test at Broadlands, Hampshire, in the early 1970s, when it was possible to catch three or more salmon in a single day's leisurely fishing. In those days the catches for each season were numbered in the hundreds. Today, the same beats at Broadlands produce fewer than fifty fish a season. The same is true of the Hampshire Avon, a river that once produced large salmon in high quantities. In those days Avon salmon had to weigh 30lb to be classed as a good fish, and an early season 40-pounder was a regular occurrence. Every season the first Avon salmon was traditionally auctioned among the local hoteliers. The occasional large salmon still falls to the traditional yellow-belly minnow of the Avon, but the big runs of prime fish have gone, probably forever.

Early season on the Avon is a cold time. The fields around the river are flat and without cover, and the wind, whatever direction it comes from, cuts like a knife. I can remember one vicious March morning when the river looked leaden and discouraging. The wind was from the northeast, and the early morning fields were white with frost. By the time I had made up my tackle my fingers were frozen, and I knew that by mid-morning I would be off to sit by the fire of a riverside pub, where the talk would invariably be about fishing. Still, I had travelled to fish an allocated day and fish I would. On that day I was on the top weirpool of the famous Royalty Fishery, a renowned pool on a top salmon fishery. Early-season Avon salmon seldom take the fly. Instead the best method is to use a buoyant wooden minnow on an elaborate paternoster rig. The 1oz lead holds the bottom while the light-bodied minnow rides high off the bottom, spinning madly in the seaward rush of the river. Those Avon minnows are works of art. Custom-made, their fat little bodies are carefully painted and varnished. The two top colours are blue and silver or, even better, browny red, with a vivid yellow belly. They look good in the hand and, more importantly, they drive salmon mad.

The technique is simple. The angler starts at the head of the pool by casting into mid-river. Once the lead weight touches bottom, the rod is lifted at regular intervals so that the bait works steadily bankwise in a huge semi-circle. At the end of each searching cast, the angler takes a long pace forwards, and the process is repeated, so that the whole of the pool area can be systematically covered.

By the end of my third cast I was so cold I was thinking of calling it quits. Then, with less than a yard of fishable water left, a salmon struck the wildly spinning minnow. This take was a typical double knock, followed instantly by a heavy pull. I do not recall striking the fish, but I do remember the first scalding run that took it to the far side of the pool and dangerously close to a downstream island. That island lay in mid-river, and because I was on the left-hand bank I was afraid that the fish would decide to run downstream via the right-hand channel around the island. I had no way to cross the river, so I simply applied maximum rod pressure and prayed. For a while the fish hung there, then it made an upstream rush towards the white foam of weir water. This gave me the opportunity to gain line and exert greater direct rod pressure. In those days we used 10ft split-cane spinning rods, and I can still hear the tortured rod creaking and the line singing under a pressure that was well beyond the call of duty. Twice the fish rolled, showing its broad silver sides. Not once did it jump. Instead it was content to make long savage runs that took it to every corner of the pool. Once I actually felt the line grate on a submerged snag, but fortunately it instantly freed itself. By now I had forgotten the cold in my hands. What I wanted was to bring that fish within gaffing range. I could sense that the fish was wearing down, and I could feel that the end was in sight. Abruptly it was over, and the fish rolled slowly on its side. Gaffing was easy, and the fish was soon out and away from the river. Minutes later I was back at the fish hut for weighing. At 31lb it was, and still is, my best-ever salmon – a fish silver flanked and with fresh sea lice. The biting chill of the wind instantly forgotten, I returned to the river. Like all anglers who have caught one fish, hopes of a brace quickly form. Needless to say, I did not achieve my greedy ambition. The river had rewarded me with one magnificent fish, and it certainly was not intending to give me another.

I have caught Atlantic salmon in Norway, Scotland, Ireland and North America. I have taken them on fly and on spinning tackle, and in Ireland I have trolled them on Lough Melvin. I would like to fish the rivers of Iceland and of the Kola Peninsula, which seem at present to be overstocked and underfished. I have heard of a party of five anglers who spent just six days on the Kola Peninsula, during which time they took and released ninety-nine salmon. These fish, which ranged from 9 to 16lb, all fell to fly rods. Several were even taken on floating flies. Alaska is another paradise for salmon anglers. King salmon, reds and cohos all seem to swarm in these icy regions. Expeditions to these far-flung salmon rivers are costly, of course, and this would seem to be the sad fact facing salmon fishermen today. Our own rivers are denuded, and unless a miracle occurs the situation will worsen. The only real chance of consistent salmon sport is to spend the money that a once-good salmon beat would cost. If the fish will not come to the angler, the angler must go to the fish. If catching a salmon is a long-felt want, do it now, before it is too late.

7
NORTHERN PIKE

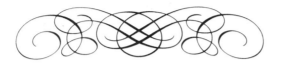

COMMON ON BOTH sides of the Atlantic, the northern pike (*Esox lucius*) is a large and popular species, found in both rivers and lakes. Totally predatory, the pike lives a solitary existence, feeding on fish of all kinds, including other pike, and also swimming rodents, frogs and even the young of various waterfowl. By natural history standards the pike is a survivor. It has existed for at least 20,000,000 years, and fossil remains show that today's pike is almost identical to its long-extinct forebear, *Esox lepidotus*.

The largest pike are found in the lochs of Scotland, the loughs of southern Ireland and in sub-alpine waters of Germany and Switzerland, and in the right conditions European pike can reach weights in excess of 50lb. In American or Canadian waters the pike is more numerous but it is usually considerably smaller. By nature, the pike is a skulker, hunting by ambush and taking up position in aquatic weeds to wait patiently for a shoal of bait fish to swim within striking range. Built for speed over short distances, the pike is quick to take advantage of an easy meal. Small to medium-sized pike live almost exclusively on live fish, and it is only later, when they grow larger and possibly slower, that they supplement their diet by scavenging. These big fish fall readily to dead fresh- or saltwater fish lying on the bed of the lake or river. American anglers seldom use natural baits for northern pike, preferring instead to use spinners, plugs, and even flies for pike fishing. In Europe, although a few anglers fish artificial lures, the majority prefer to fish with live or dead fish. The difference is that in North America the waters are vast and there are more pike. In Europe there are fewer fish, the waters are far smaller, and the anglers are more numerous and concentrated – in short, there are not enough fish nor enough space to wander at will with a spinning or fly rod.

By New World standards fly-rodding for northern pike is the most exciting way of catching these fish. The ideal place to use a fly is in the weedy shallows, where the fish can often be seen before they snap up the fly. A pike fly is much larger than the flies used for trout or salmon, and most of the successful patterns are tied on the streamer principle, with each fly tied to imitate a small fish. These streamer patterns are tied on size 3–0 hooks and each fly is 5–6in long. As an alternative, some anglers use cork-bodied bass poppers, which chug busily across the surface. Northern pike will often go mad on these unlikely looking baits.

It is important to choose the right outfit for fly-rodding. Most anglers fish from boats and use an 8ft 6in or a 9ft rod that is capable of casting an 8 or 9 weight-forward floating line. The reel must be large enough to hold a full fly line, plus at least 100 yards of 20lb b.s. Dacron backing line. The leaders should be tied from lengths of 30, 25, 20, 15 and 12lb nylon, and the tippet should be 12in of 30lb b.s. nylon. Some anglers prefer very short, flexible, wire tippets, but these can make casting difficult. Fly colour is difficult to establish. One day the pike will go for red and white streamers, the next day they seem to prefer another colour. For this reason it is advisable to tie up a selection of flies in different colour combinations.

Popular as it is, fly-fishing for northern pike is still a minority sport compared to spin-fishing with spoons and plugs. This is the fun-fishing side of North American pike fishing, whose devotees use short, 7ft long, pistol-gripped graphite bait-casters, the latest in ever-developing reel technology, and a cantilevered lure box, crammed with a dazzling variety of plugs and spinners. Originally hand-carved to represent small fish, plug baits are now mass-produced. The early hand-carved plugs now have a high antique value, and they feature prominently in specialist fishing tackle auctions. Some of the early tried and trusted plugs, like the Creek Chub Pikie and the original Rapala pattern, are still made and sold, but in many cases wood has given way to plastic, and baits are churned out by the million from modern injection-moulding machines. New designs and finishes appear almost daily and, unless they are careful, anglers can start with a few baits and end up with a collection costing thousands of dollars.

Spinning and plug-fishing is a fascinating way of taking northern pike. Most of the fishing is done from a drifting boat, and the cast is made so that the lure works the shorelines thoroughly and the first drop-off sections of the water are fished. This is a peaceful form of fishing, allowing the angler to come into full contact with nature. Often the only sound is the whirring of the reel spool or the screech of a ratchet as a well-hooked fish plunges away. North American waters are clear and cold, and the actions of hooked fish can usually be clearly seen. A hooked pike will often jump in a glistening spray of white water. Once played out, the fish is normally netted. Experienced pike anglers may use a pair of long-nosed pliers to release the hooks while the fish is still in the water, but this technique can be dangerous, and many anglers have ended their day at the hospital, having hooks removed or stitches put into deep gashes caused by the pike's teeth.

All anglers like to catch big fish but North American anglers are content to take what comes and to count a good day by the numbers, not the size, of fish caught. European anglers, on the other hand, are very big-fish conscious, and they will go to extreme lengths to avoid small to medium-sized pike, which is another reason why lure-fishing is not widely practised in European waters. With the exception of some of the larger lakes, lochs and loughs, boat-fishing for pike is not common, with anglers preferring wherever possible to fish from the shore out-wards rather than from the lake shorewards. Much European pike fishing is done on lakes that would be regarded as little more than puddles by anglers from North America. Many of these 'puddles' are on private estates, where the lakes were hand dug to provide fish for the landowner, but the limited size of these often beautiful little lakes means that the angler is lim-ited to one section of bank. This fact, coupled with the anglers' desire to catch only a big fish, means that a totally different style of angling has evolved. Artificial lures and lightweight spin-fishing outfits are out. In their place come a pair of 12–13ft cast-ing rods, large fixed-spool reels, a comfortable chair and a pair of electronic bite alarms. River anglers may do away with one rod, the chair and the alarms, and carry a bucket filled with live bait fish, which are kept alive by a small battery-operated aerator. The lake-angler rarely uses live bait because it attracts too many small pike. The target here is a fish of 30lb or more. It is amazing how large pike can grow in lakes with a total surface area of less than 10 acres. All that seems to matter to the pike is that there is comparatively deep water and that the food supply is plentiful.

Few lakes are of uniform depth, and pike tend to use the deeper gullies as patrol areas. By thoroughly plumbing and charting the contours of a lake bed, the angler can place baits in the most potentially productive areas. Long casts are often essential. These casts, which would kill a live fish, can be easily achieved by the use of a suitably sized dead fish. The three most widely used dead baits are mackerel, smelt and herring. It may sound strange to use sea fish as bait for a freshwater species, but the pike do not seem to care, and they often take a sea fish in preference to a dead trout or other freshwater species. Mackerel, used whole or cut in half, is the bait to use for long-casting purposes. Scavenging pike show just as much interest in cut baits as in whole baits. Herring is a good pike bait, but it does not stand up to distance casting and is best used for short-range fishing. Smelt casts well and has the added advantage of giving off a strong cucumber-like odour, a smell that pike seem to find particularly attractive. No matter what dead bait is used the terminal tackle remains unchanged: a braided line, 18in long and of 20 or 25lb b.s., with a small barrel swivel at one end and a size 6 or 8 barbless treble hook at the other. Between these is a single size 4 hook, which is simply used to support the bait during casting. One prong of the treble hook should be stuck into the dead bait near to the gill plate, with the support hook in the root of the bait's tail. No additional lead is needed, the weight of the bait being sufficient for casting purposes.

Once cast out, the line is tightened so that it sinks, and the rod is then placed in a pair of rod rests, with a visual or a complex electronic indicator used to detect bites. The reel is usually of the Shimano baitrunner type, which will give line easily to a taking pike. Two sets of identical tackle are used to present two baits to a cruising fish. At best this is a slow, contemplative form of angling, which gives the angler plenty of time to take in the scenery and passing bird life. Once a fish is hooked, it is played out and netted in the conventional manner. The barbless treble hook is then removed with surgical forceps, and the fish is carefully weighed and returned as quickly as possible to the water. By North American standards this may sound a rather dreary, inactive way of taking fish, but European anglers are interested only in catching the biggest pike in the water, and static fishing with large dead baits has proved to be the best way to achieve this ambition. On a bright autumn day, when the leaves have turned and are beginning to fall, a day spent quietly at the side of a lovely lake has much to recommend it, and this must be one reason why autumn and winter pike fishing is so popular with European anglers.

8
BLACK BASS

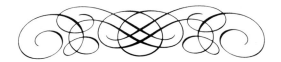

EVERY INCH AN American fish, the small-mouthed bass (*Micropterus dolomieui*) and the large-mouthed bass (*M. salmoides*) are the favourite target species for most American freshwater anglers. Over half a million anglers belong to BASS (Bass Anglers Sportsman Society), and many thousands more belong to other bass clubs and chapters. Their whole fishing lives are given over to catching, recording, releasing and promoting bass fishing in all its aspects. Mammoth tournaments are regularly organized, offering huge prizes to tempt and encourage more and better anglers to enter the highly professional tournament circuit. Many anglers become full-time professionals, following the tournaments on a year-round basis, and not only do these top anglers win a great deal of money, they also earn from 'spin-off' industries by putting their names to tackle, clothing, shoes and boats. Of the six recognized types of bass, the large-mouthed is the most popular species. It has a wider geographical range than the small-mouthed bass, and it reaches a much greater size. Small-mouthed bass tournaments do exist, but they do not get the publicity or the following enjoyed by the large-mouthed bass contests.

Large-mouthed bass are giant members of the Centrarchidae or sunfish family, a group of fish that is found only in North America and consists of thirty species. These range from 1½in-long Everglades pygmy sunfish on up to the large-mouthed bass, which can top 20lb in weight. The name bass is said to come from the old English word *baers*, which means 'bristly' or 'spiky', and this is certainly an apt description of the first dorsal fin. The bass is a dumpy fish, built for agility rather than speed, and it is very much a species of still waters – transplanted large-mouthed bass seldom do well in running water. The bass is a surface-feeder, the large mouth

intercepting just about anything edible or seemingly edible that enters its domain. When a good-sized bass slams into a surface-running lure, it usually takes on the jump, crashing out in a flurry of foam, with the bait clamped firmly in its jaws.

Large-mouthed bass have been widely transplanted, and many man-made waters have been selectively stocked with the Florida strain of large-growing bass. The fish seem to thrive in the southern and western states – Texas, California, Florida, Georgia and South Carolina have all produced numerous bass of 15lb or more in weight – and bass fishing has achieved such a following that the State of Georgia actually unveiled a marker to commemorate the catching of a 22lb 4oz record bass from Lake Montgomery. The lake that consistently produces big bass for local and visiting anglers is Lake Okeechobee in Florida, which is the fourth largest natural lake in the USA.

Bass fishing in the USA has become something of a science, and the big-money tournaments have created a huge demand for all types of bass fishing tackle. Like all anglers, bass fishermen have their likes and dislikes. Some fly-fish only; others restrict their angling techniques to plug-fishing. In recent years the bait-making industry has come up with a astounding selection of moulded rubber baits. These lures, which are moulded in a soft rubber that feels almost like the live creature it is designed to represent, are sold in the shapes of worms, frogs, salamanders and so forth, and they come in a staggering variety of colours, all of which catch fish on their day. The fly-fishing fanatics tend to use streamer flies and surface poppers.

The plug enthusiasts are probably the most versatile anglers of the three camps. Plugs are available as floaters, sinkers and deep divers. Floating plugs are designed to wiggle along on the surface, and they are widely used for taking bass from pockets of water surrounded by weeds. Sinking plugs are used for fishing deepish runs close to dense weedbeds. The deep-diving plugs are designed to search out big bass in deep water. The faster the angler cranks the reel handle, the deeper the plug dives, and in the hands of an expert these deep-running plugs can be used to search out every hole and drop-off in a bass lake. Plug-anglers are never satisfied with a bait straight from the shop or factory, however. They invariably get to work with a pair of pliers, tweaking the bait's diving lip until the lure is thoroughly tuned to their satisfaction. It is this close attention to detail that wins tournaments, and with many thousands of dollars and often big prizes at stake, nothing is left to chance. Many top tournament anglers make their own plugs, secret weapons that are seldom shown to other anglers, and these home-made baits achieve legendary status in tournament circles.

A fascinating aspect of the American pro-bass circuit is that the publicity it has generated has led to large-mouthed bass being stocked in many other countries. Black bass are now stocked in the southern half of the Iberian peninsula, and the fish are now common in the vast mountain *lavadas* or reservoirs of Portugal. Here, they are mostly fished with live baits on fly rods. Zimbabwe in southern Africa has been extensively stocked with black bass from the southern USA. In some areas the bass have been stocked behind large dams, in others they have gone directly into natural lakes. So successful has the policy been, that thriving bass chapters have been set up, and this has led to many tournaments between chapters from different districts. These are run on American pro-bass rules, and they take place every weekend throughout the dry season.

I was fortunate to be invited to participate in an important tournament on Lake McIllwane, outside the capital city, Harare. The fishing was to take place on a Saturday, with everyone arriving on the Friday afternoon. All the members of the Harare bass chapter share in the cost of running a full-time bar, and all members provide the food. The mainstay of the menu is roast ox, washed down by endless beers. Everyone sleeps under canvas, and fishing starts early. The lake is large, with vast areas of weedy shallows that are ideal for both black bass and huge crocodiles. The fishing is done from boats, all of which, with their outboard and electric bow motors, are imported directly from the USA. The same goes for the tackle. All tackle is difficult to obtain in Zimbabwe, but the bass fanatic will obtain the new state-of-the-art gear by hook or by crook.

Tournaments start at 7 o'clock and finish at 4 o'clock. Every fish caught is kept alive and, wherever possible, returned alive to the water after being carefully weighed. Some of the largest bass lurk in the thickest weed, and this makes fishing with surface-running lures fun. When a bass spots the moving bait, it surges up out of the weed on a seek-and-destroy mission. The plug bait simply vanishes in a mighty explosion of weed and water. Zimbabwe bass hit and fight like their ancestors from the deep south of the USA. One second nothing, then that incredible feeling of the rod dragging down as a big, angry bass puts on a show of savage pulling power and frenzied jumping. During the course of a day on Lake McIllwane miles of rich and varied shoreline are covered, and every weedbed, lily patch and hole is thoroughly searched.

Finally, late in the afternoon, the bow motors are lifted and the big outboards roar into life, taking everyone back to the camp for the weigh in, huge sandwiches, thick with roasted ox meat, and endless cans of the heady African beer, served straight from the freezer. No matter how hot the late African sun gets, these Zimbabwe bass men know how to keep their cool. Although the rivalry between the teams is intense, the whole day has an air of great enjoyment. The anglers fish; their families stay ashore and treat each weekend as a magic holiday. The bass clubs have their own centres, where members and visiting anglers can drop in during the week in and talk fishing, such is the love of black bass fishing.

Anglers in southern Africa dream about fishing in Florida; American anglers go to Zimbabwe and fish with bass men who are as keen as they are. Large-mouthed or small-mouthed bass are fish worthy of any angler's time. Their prowess as a fighting species and their liking for a wide variety of lures, plugs and plastic baits makes this species unique. The fish can be caught on totally artificial lures, which puts them within range of those anglers whose conservationist policies do not allow the use of live fish, frogs or worms. What is even more interesting, however, is that the use of today's artificial lures has created an interest in the baits and tackle of yesteryear. Many anglers start out just wanting to catch black bass, but in the process they become aware of antique bass tackle. Normally, this awareness leads to the angler becoming a collector of vintage bass tackle and baits – one interest instantly becomes two, and the bass fisher becomes an angler and a collector. Such is the power of bass fishing. Already a massive industry in the USA, bass angling is set to take much of the world by storm and long may its popularity increase. The black bass is a dream fish for the light tackle angler. It is a fighting species, akin to trout and salmon in spirit, and it must be hoped that the enthusiasm for bass fishing will increase as stocking policies extend the range of this magnificent species.

9
TIGER FISH

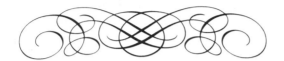

BEYOND KARIBA TOWNSHIP the vast expanse of Lake Kariba lay glass-flat in the hot Zimbabwean sun. Far away, an indistinct blue line showed the Matusadonna Mountains and one of the greatest tiger fish hot-spots in Africa. Two hours later the first ski-boat ferry was nosing into the rocks below Sanyati lodge. This fish camp is situated in the Matusadonna range, less than half a mile from where the deep green waters of the River Sanyati merge with the blue-grey waters of the Kariba and its inflowing rivers, which hold over forty species of fish. These range from the tiny minnow-like kapinta, through to the mighty vundu catfish, which can reach weights of several hundred pounds. Only the sabre-toothed, high-leaping tiger fish is of interest to anglers, however. The tiger fish, which is similar in appearance to fish of the South American characin family, was left behind when the two land masses first drifted apart, and it is now found in the various rivers of Zimbabwe and Botswana and is also common in Lake Kariba.

There are five species of tiger fish. The commonest, *Hydrocyon lineatus*, reaches weights of 30–40lb, and although the goliath tiger fish (*Hydrocyon goliath*) of the Congo River system can double this weight, it does not seem to have the speed, temper or manoeuvrability of the smaller species. Totally predatory, the tiger fish feeds on young fish of many kinds, and adult fish are happy to eat young of their own kind. On the Kariba and its adjoining rivers the kapinta fish is the mainstay of its diet. Kapinta are an introduced species which have become a major food source for the tribesmen on both the Zambian and Zimbabwean sides of the lake. The 6,000 square miles of water held in Lake Kariba have provided the kapinta shoals with rich spawning grounds, on which both the tiger fish and the hundreds of giant kapinta boats operate round the clock.

Tiger fish can be caught by spinning, trolling, on natural bait and sometimes on fly rods. The really big fish are normally taken by trolling a large lure behind a slow-moving boat. Like all the world's fishing grounds Kariba has its noted big fish areas, and the River Sanyati is the place to tangle with a monster tiger fish. Fishing in Africa starts early and late. From late morning until late afternoon is lunch and siesta time, the full heat of the African sun being more than man or beast can take. A typical day at Sanyati starts at 4.30 in the morning with a cup of tea and a light breakfast. Then it is down the mountain in the dark to load the tackle into the waiting boats. As dawn breaks, the engines start and the boats make their way out into the lake through a forest of drowned trees, and on to the dark mouth and the green roily water of the River Sanyati. This is wild Africa at its best. The rocks rise high and grey before scrub trees and bush take over. Here are the lairs of the leopard, the fish eagle and the basking crocodile. It is a beautiful, dangerous river canyon, haunted by tribal superstition. A fitting place to catch a tiger fish.

For those anglers who want a really big tiger fish, the first half mile inside the river mouth is the place to be. Here the water runs at its deepest and greenest, and it is here that the big tiger fish come to

hunt in solitary splendour. Trolling is the technique to use; the lure a deep-running Rapala plug or a big, green-backed copper or silver spinner. The trick is to let the bait run far back from the slowly moving boat; when a strike comes, the fish is either instantly hooked or just as instantly lost. The original treble hooks of the spoon bait should have been replaced with a large, carefully sharpened, size 6–0 single hook. Tiger fish have savage, lip-mounted, interlocking teeth, and while a single hook may lodge in solid flesh between this barrage of teeth, a treble has no chance to do this and should, therefore, be discarded. Once hooked, big tiger fish will turn and take line at speed. At first, they head downwards in search of a sanctuary. When this fails, they may resort to a surface battle. The big Kariba fish are too heavy to jump seriously, but they will put on a tail-waving display of raw temper that has to be seen to be believed.

Trying to catch one of these outsized fish is an all-or-nothing venture. You might get lucky on the first morning, or you might fish for a week without touching one. For many anglers there are too many blank hours involved in this kind of fishing. They come to Sanyati to catch tiger fish and size is not everything. Fortunately, the middle and upper reaches of the Sanyati gorge are packed with small and medium-sized fish, which can be taken by spin- or fly-casting from a drifting boat or by casting artificial or natural baits from a boat tied to bankside vegetation. What these smaller tiger fish lack in weight, they more than make up for in savageness. They take the bait or lure with a rod-wrenching slam and instantly become airborne. They do not jump as much as cartwheel in a welter of flying spray. Not once will they admit defeat, even attempting to jump when netted. Catches are high, and every rod may get twelve to twenty fish in a morning or evening session, each fish seemingly stronger and more ferocious than its predecessor. This is wonderful, lovely sport, where the fish hit hard amid magnificent scenery. The rich and vivid bird life of the river is a constant spectacle – soaring fish eagles, yellow-billed kites, a host of varied kingfishers and the rare African finfoot can be seen every day in the gorge. If you are really lucky, you may also catch more than a glimpse of a flock of carmine bee-eaters, surely one of Africa's most beautiful small birds.

Lake Kariba with its inflowing rivers is just one place to catch fighting tiger fish. The River Zambezi is another must for the visitor wanting to catch tiger fish. Long-standing fans of the tiger fish rather pour scorn on the lake fish, claiming that Kariba tiger fish are too fat to fight hard. Zambezi fish, on the other hand, spend their lives battling against savage currents, and they will consequently out-fight their lake cousins, no matter what tackle is used. Tiger fish in the River Zambezi are certainly lean and muscular, and they are more capable of pulling their weight in a battle. Their style is different, however. Large Kariba tiger fish dive when they are hooked. In the Zambezi the fish simply do not have the depth of water to go deep. Instead, they turn and run for 50, 60, even 100 yards, then surface in a series of heart-stopping leaps. Fly-fishing is seldom practised in the coloured waters of the Zambezi. The technique is, instead, to spin, troll or bait-fish. Hooks, as always, are carefully sharpened singles, and, as always, a strong wire trace is essential.

Fish and game camps are plentiful on the upper Zambezi, one of the best being Imbabala camp, 60 miles upstream of Victoria Falls, where the river is wide and broken up by many large and small islands, home to surly, aggressive hippo, hosts of elephants and multitudes of water birds. Large crocodiles are common, but they are rarely seen, and the hippopotamus is regarded as potentially the most dangerous of the river animals. Imbabala camp fishes early and late, and it is easy to catch big tiger fish in the morning and to go out to watch elephants and lions in the late afternoon. The Zambezi is at its most beautiful in the early morning. The air is fresh and cool, and the river is alive with the splashes of feeding tiger fish. The fishing is done in the main river, where the water flow is savage and every bankside tree holds a multitude of white herons. This is a wild section of river. The fishing is unpredictable, and the tiger packs follow the schools of bait fish, which sometimes forsake the main flow for the lily-covered backwaters. This is dangerous but productive country, where hippo packs lounge in tranquillity until a boat appears. Then a cow with calf or a bull hippo may charge and charge again in an attempt to drive off or destroy the offending visitor.

Copper spoons are the big fish-catchers on the river – for some reason, other colours seem to hold little fish appeal – and the top fish-catcher is a heavy 3in wobbling spoon, rather than a revolving spoon. The theory is that the wobbling, copper-coloured lure closely resembles a small local species of bream, which is much favoured by the ever-hungry tiger fish. Zambezi tigers hit a lure solidly. For every fish hooked, three of more bounce off, and, although this can be frustrating at first, once a fish is hooked its power and raw strength make up for earlier losses. For an angler to go to Africa and not fish for tiger fish is an unthinkable omission. Beware, however, for once you are hooked, Africa and its tigers are a magnet that will draw you back many times.

10
NILE PERCH

LAKE VICTORIA ON a hot pre-dawn African morning. Early water birds are flighting to the shallow feeding grounds, and the vast lake lies like a steel mirror, awaiting the blistering heat of the day to come. Far out in the lake a fish rolls, but it is not just any fish – this is the great Nile perch (*Lates niloticus*), a monster of a fish, capable of reaching weights in excess of 200lb. This is the sort of fish that brings anglers from all over the world. It may not be the greatest of all the fighting species, but it is a big fish to tackle on a beefed-up set of spinning tackle. The Nile perch of Lake Turkana in Uganda probably grow bigger than the Lake Victoria fish, but Turkana does not have the same facilities and is further to travel. Much of the fishing on Lake Victoria is done from Rusinga Island, one of the few places where there is an active fish camp. Africa wakes early and the fishing is often at its best soon after dawn. To be out on a water the size of Lake Victoria just as the sun rises is an experience in itself. Flights of waterfowl pass over head *en route* to their feeding grounds, and the lake surface is a hive of fish activity as tiny bait fish scatter to the splash of plundering perch. The sort of activity that almost guarantees you good fishing to come.

Like all big fish, the Nile perch has its favoured feeding areas, usually at a point where the marginal shallows fall away into deeper water. This drop-off point is regularly patrolled by the hunting perch, for the fish know that the shallows are alive with small bait fish, and they wait for some straying individual to venture too close to the deep water. The pickings in such places are rich, and the Nile perch grow quickly in Lake Victoria, a sure sign of an abundant food supply.

Nile perch can be caught on live or dead fish or on large, well-polished spinners. The experts, however, prefer to fish the plug, and every successful Nile perch angler has his or her favourite plug baits.

Some anglers even go to the trouble of making up specials, intricate, hand-carved lures that their owners and makers claim will catch fish when all the shop-bought patterns fail. The truth of the matter is that you must have faith and confidence in your lure selection – then and only then will your plug baits catch fish. All the lures by the top manufacturers can be relied on to produce strikes, and on its day Rapalas, Rebels, Creek Chub or any other big, well-actioned plug will take

fish. Nile perch are not fussy feeders, and they will hit any lure with colour and a good action. The Nile perch boats carry a selection of plugs, and most of these are rather battered because a big perch, weighing more than 100lb, hits a lure like a freight train. Each bout of action leaves its own series of scars and digs on the bait's body.

Heavy spinning or light boat rods are about right for Nile perch, with the choice of reel being up to the individual angler. Most choose medium-sized multiplying reels with either a lever or a star-drag system. Despite their huge size, Nile perch are not strong fighters and can be easily caught on lines of 20 or 25lb b.s. The smaller fish, weighing up to 50 or 60lb, normally fight on the surface, often in full view of the angler. The really large specimens, which are normally females, tend to be more sluggish and prefer to stay in deep water.

Interestingly, the ancient Egyptians fished for Nile perch over 4,500 years ago. In one burial tomb there is a mural of two men carrying a Nile perch suspended from a paddle. The hieroglyphic inscription above the painting reads 'capturing the aha fish'. Obviously then, as now, the local population used these big fish as a good source of protein. During the early part of this century fishing for Nile perch was a favourite pastime with the Europeans working in Africa. The tackle used in those days was extremely basic: heavy greenheart or split-cane rods, Hardy Silex centre-pins and braided line, which had a tendency to rot in the humidity of Africa. Most of the fishing was done with live bait or slowly trolled dead baits. Despite the inadequate tackle, fish to 200lb were successfully landed. The tackle used today is light, easy to handle and near perfect for Nile perch fishing. Live and dead bait-fishing is now very much a thing of the past, trolling being the best method to use. The beauty of trolling is that it shows the lures over a wide area while covering a variety of potential hot-spots *en route*. This in itself makes for interesting fishing, because the angler has the additional privilege of viewing local wild life along the banks. Venturing out on a vast African lake as dawn breaks is a wonderful experience. There is a magical sense of anticipation, and this is heightened by the sights and smells of truly wild places. The grunt of a hippo, the slithery splash of a crocodile, the tang of muddy water and decaying weed – all these things unite to create an animated picture of the day ahead.

The fishing technique is simple. The skipper of the boat heads directly for known areas of shallow water, where the boat is kept on a course dictated by the meanderings of the drop-off into deep water. Large Nile perch frequently invade the shallows during the hours of darkness, dropping back as the light grows in intensity. The angler's aim is to intercept the giant fish as they leave the shallows, and this is why the first hours of daylight are often the most productive fishing times. Normally two, occasionally four, anglers share a boat. Two is ideal, because four can lead to tangles. The big plug baits are attached to heavy nylon traces joined to the reel line by a swivel. The plugs are designed to dive and waggle well beneath the surface. Like all predatory fish, Nile perch have days when they favour one style or colour of plug over another, but, above all, a good plug that runs true and works well will usually attract fish if there are any about. Some anglers like to hold their rods, others prefer to wedge them into rod holders with the drag system of the reel being lightly set to give line the second a fish hits a lure. Nile perch are not subtle feeders. Once they sight a bait they want, they simply surge up behind it, open their enormous mouth, and suck it in. Most fish hook themselves on impact, but the smaller fish seem confused when hooked. Although the occasional fish will make a long run, most content themselves with short runs, culminating in a lot of splashy surface activity. Some of the big fish may take a lot of line, using bulk rather than fighting ability to apply pressure, but the fight is seldom sustained. The hardest part of the battle is to work the fish to the surface. There was a time when all Nile perch were caught and killed, but conservation-minded fishermen can now operate on a catch-and-release basis. A really big fish can, of course, be brought ashore for weighing, but the smaller specimens are best released alive. As a sport Nile perch fishing is enjoying a growing reputation. Anglers from all over the world visit Africa in the hope of catching one of the world's largest freshwater fish. Fortunately, the Nile perch is an obliging species, so few anglers go away disappointed.

11
BLUEFIN TUNA

THE BLUEFIN TUNA (*Thunnus thynnus*) is the largest and most powerful of the tuna tribe, and has long been high on the big game fisherman's hit list. Its sheer size and indisputable strength making it a spectacular fish to see and catch. Unfortunately, it is also a good fish to eat, and its raw, cooked and pickled flesh is in great demand in the markets and fish restaurants of Japan, where it commands an increasingly high price.

Since records began the bluefin tuna has been a well-documented fish and the basis of some interesting legends. Polybius (205–125 BC) wrote: 'The tuna wander through the deep of the sea to a place where an oak tree grows. There they gorge themselves on acorns until they become so obese that they explode.' Aristotle (384–322 BC) noted that the 'sea pig' gorges until it reaches a weight of 15 talents (roughly 1,200lb). The acorns and exploding theory obviously caught the imagination, and it was commonly quoted until the late Middle Ages. For the time this was a reasonable explanation for the fact that some years giant tuna were abundant, yet in other years they appeared to have vanished from the seas, a situation that prevails today. Whether the great shoals of those long-past days suffered some strange disease we cannot know, but what we do know is that, today, the tuna is being harried off the face of the world's oceans by the increasing demand for its flesh.

Tuna certainly have a strange habit of vanishing from areas where they were once prolific. In the 1930s the North Sea off Scarborough, Yorkshire, England, was the place to catch a giant tuna. One of the top English exponents of rod-and-line fishing for bluefin was Mitchell-Henry, who at one time held the world record for the species with a monster taken from the North Sea. From the 1930s until the early 1950s English anglers went to sea with the herring

fleet, then transferred to small boats to fish a freshly dead herring close to where loose herring spilled from the herring nets as they were hauled. This was a rough, tough sport with tackle that by today's standards was primitive and heavy. It was this fishing that prompted Hardy to produce its range of Fortuna reels, which are now avidly sought after by collectors of antique fishing tackle. It is interesting that the huge reels produced in Britain followed the traditional centre-pin design. In the USA these reels held little appeal for anglers, who instead preferred the multiplying reel. For a while it was Britain against America in the quest for bigger and bigger bluefin. Then the bubble burst. The stocks of North Sea herring were depleted by over-fishing and, with the passing of the bait fish, the mighty bluefins vanished in the space of two seasons.

By this stage American anglers, too, had experienced the phenomenon of disappearing tuna. Wedge Port, Nova Scotia, once described as the bluefin capital of the world, lost its fish at approximately the same time as Europe's North Sea. The fish then appeared off Newfoundland in the 1960s. Sport lasted for a decade then once again the fish moved on, this time to Prince Edward Island, New Brunswick, and the Canso Causeway linking Nova Scotia to Breton Island. The first 1,000-pounder – to be exact 1,065lb – was taken off an area close to the Canso Causeway in November 1970. Since that first monster, hundreds of 1,000-pounders have been taken from the same area. The records have increased to nearly 1,500lb and could easily go higher.

Back in the 1930s Bimini in the Bahamas was a great tuna hotspot. Fish were taken by the hundred, and for every one brought into the boat many more were lost. These were the days when Ernest Hemingway spent the May and June of most years at Bimini. These were the days of experimentation, when skippers became legends and tuna fishing techniques were perfected. The late Tommy Gifford developed the art of kite-fishing for tuna. The angler's line is loosely attached to the kite, leaving the bait and hook dangling freely beneath it. Gifford then worked the kite so that the bait actually skipped from wave top to wave top, and the rampaging tuna chased the fast-moving bait. Kite-fishing brought about the downfall of many a monster bluefin. Tuna still run the Bahama banks, but not in the way they once did. Early sport-fishing took its toll, but the money paid by the Tokyo fish market must take much of the blame.

Today, the story is the same everywhere – bluefin stocks are in savage decline wherever these wonderful fish occur. Even so, as long as you know where to go, there are still enough of them to provide the occasional bout of hot fishing. Bluefin are found throughout the world, but the largest are taken in the western Atlantic. They are thick-bodied, heavily muscled fish, so heavily muscled, in fact, that the blood temperature is often 5–10 degrees higher than the ambient seawater. In an ideal world, bluefin can live for approximately thirty years. Fast-moving, voracious predators, they hunt small fish, squid and cuttle-fish, and, although they are normally regarded as surface-feeders, the stomach contents of adult bluefin indicate that on occasion they hunt in the depths of the ocean. Pacific bluefin are not as large as their Atlantic cousins. The California records start at a mere 363½lb – a tiddler by eastern seaboard standards.

The legendary Zane Grey triggered the passion for bluefin fishing. In 1924 Grey caught a 758-pounder off Nova Scotia. One American angler actually 'took' no fewer than 642 giant tuna during his fishing lifetime. On his best day his haul was sixteen fish! Ann Kunnel, an angler from Palm Beach, Florida, caught no fewer than 110 monster bluefin, of which 106 were tagged and released. I recall meeting Mrs Kunnel at a Walker's Cay tournament. Her big game fishing days were over, but she still relished the exuberance of a major tournament.

I have caught bluefin in the Atlantic islands and also in the Bahamas. The potentially largest one I hooked had a rather sad ending. We had been trolling in the vicinity of Matanilla Reef, an offshore hot-spot that is a noted feeding place for bluefin and white marlin. It was these fish we were out for, because no tuna had been caught or sighted for some weeks. When a giant boil of water engulfed a brightly skirted Kona Head, we knew it was a bluefin. Marlin tend to follow a bait and take it rather delicately. A bluefin, on the other hand, hits like a bomb going off. A great gout of flying water, which actually seems to leave a crater in the ocean, is the bluefin's trademark. The second the bait vanishes, the reel starts to scream as the startled monster goes into crash dive. This fish was typical: it took, felt the hook and was on its way like an express train. The big rod was so bent that I had difficulty in pulling it free of the rod pod. Once it was free, I struggled to the chair with a screaming reel clutch to remind me that I still had to get the rod butt into the chair gimbal and snap the harness clips onto the reel lugs. Under International Game Fish Association (IGFA) rules, no one can help an angler. If they do help and the fish turns out to be a record, it is instantly disqualified.

I knew from the onset that this was a monster. Lone bluefin tend to be huge, and I thought that this one might top the 1,000lb mark.

I was fishing an 80lb-class outfit, which had enough line for most fish, but an angry bluefin can take line under savage fighting pressure that no other fish could hope to conquer. Like all tuna, this one went down. Obviously it felt the sanctuary of deep, black water would ease the pain in its jaw. Fortunately, I had been this route before in the Azores, Madeira and the Canary Islands, and I knew that to try to fight the fish during its first dive would be futile. I maintained maximum drag pressure and prayed the fish would stop running before it came to the end of the line. The spool emptied fast, and when the fish slowed to a halt I estimated that there was no more than 100 yards of line left on the reel. Once stopped, a fighting tuna turns on its side to achieve maximum water pressure on its shield-shaped body. At first it is impossible to move, but after a few minutes such fish can be raised. The technique is to pile on rod pressure and to watch the rod tip. When it starts to straighten, the fish is giving ground. Soon I was gaining line, and in just over an hour the reel was half-filled with line. At this stage the fish decided enough was enough, a change of heart that cost me a lot of line, line that I was soon getting back. For two-and-a-half hours the fish went down to the mid-water level. By now I was wearing down, but then I got my second wind. The bitter part of the fight was just beginning.

At this stage in a confrontation with a big fish there is only the angler and the fish. Both are equally determined to win, and neither is prepared to give ground. At the end of three-and-a-half hours I had the fish on the move. Inch by desperate inch I was gaining ground, but then I felt a thump on the line. This was quickly followed by a series of rod-wrenching jolts, and I knew the sharks were on the great tuna. I could have thrown the rod over the side. That fish was part of me, welded for all time by memories and a strand of line. I had intended to release the magnificent fish, but now, far down below the sunlight, it was being savaged by shark. Soon enough I felt it was dead. Sadly, I cranked the reel handle to lift the inert body. I could still feel the bumping of feeding shark, but the fun was gone. Initially it had been fair combat, but now I was simply trying to save a corpse. When the great fish hit surface, the whole section from the middle of the body to the tail was missing. The sharks were still there – a brace of tiger shark and an evil-looking hammerhead. Later, the remains weighed in at 509lb, but what had once been beautiful was a ruin, a scarred mess, that no one wanted. Of all the big fish I have ever caught, this is one I shall always regret.

12
SAILFISH

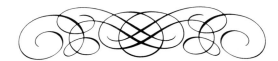

For those who wish to catch a monster sailfish (*Istiophorus platypterus*) the Pacific side of Mexico is the place to be. Here the 'sails' can weigh an average 100lb, and a big one will top the 150lb mark. On the other side of Mexico, in the seas off lovely Cozumel Island, the fish are much smaller, most weighing in at 50–70lb. What these Cozumel fish lack in weight, they more than make up for in numbers, however, and catches of fifteen to twenty 'sails' are taken a day. Without exception, all these fish are released, a conservation policy that should, one hopes, maintain the Cozumel stocks for many years to come.

This is rapidly becoming fly-rodding country, where the hunting sailfish are brought up by trolling teasers. Once a fish has been sighted, the hookless teasers are wound in and the angler casts from the drifting boat. To cast a big streamer fly to an active sailfish is one of the excitements of modern big game fishing. The tackle is a 9ft 6in or a 10ft trout rod, designed to throw a number 8 or 9 line. The reel is a Hardy Ocean Prince, a system 2 saltwater special, or a Billy Pate tarpon reel. Such a reel will take both the fly line and a minimum of 250 yards of 20lb b.s. Dacron backing. A backing line of 250 yards may sound excessive, but in practice it just melts through the rod rings as a well-hooked and angry sailfish shows its mettle. The flies for sailfish are streamer patterns, designed to imitate the natural colours of bait fish.

Most fly-fishing sail fishermen tie their own imitative patterns. Each fly is designed to trigger off the killing instinct of a fish already frustrated by the vanished teasers. The technique is to cast beyond, and ahead of, the searching sailfish. The fly, which is attached by a 25lb b.s. cast, is allowed to sink down a few feet and is stripped rapidly back, to cross the fish's line of vision. Once sighted, the fly may be intercepted at high speed or it may be carefully shadowed for many yards before the fish makes its decision. One in four fish may simply trail along, looking the fly over before sinking gently and silently from sight. Once the fish starts to close on a fly at speed, however, it will almost certainly take the lure, and, once it is hooked, its immediate reaction will be to run and jump, stripping hundreds of feet of line in the process. Constant rod pressure will keep it constantly in the air: a raw, savage, yet beautiful display of beautiful aerobatics that few fish can equal. Constant rod pressure and the sullen drag of fly line and backing will soon begin to take its toll, and the fish will forsake its surface action for a hoped-for refuge in the deep water. This is the time to pile on the pressure. The sailfish relies on savage surface action to get it out of trouble, and, when jumping and running fail to dislodge the drag of hook and line, its nerve begins to go. Its only sanctuary is the deep water, but this is not its natural habitat, and the fish begins to crack. Soon it will begin to circle deep down, losing yard after yard of precious ground to the angler. Finally, it will come up, tired and exhausted but still with its magnificent sail held high and the defiance still in its lovely eyes. The fish comes in expecting death, but then its bill is held, the fly is removed and one of nature's loveliest fish is released, to live and breed in the vastness of the ocean. For the angler this is often the part of the battle that will be remembered forever. That last glimpse of the slim bill-fish, with its vast, brightly coloured sail is a difficult memory to erase. Take and release a Cozumel Island sailfish, and you will automatically join the élite branch of the big game fishing world.

Interestingly, the practice of fly-fishing for sailfish is spreading. On the coast of Kenya, where the sailfish runs are huge, local and visiting anglers are combining information in the hope of promoting sailfish in fly-rod tournaments. Like Cozumel, the lovely coast of Kenya is a mecca for sailfish fishermen, and, from October through to March, huge numbers of sailfish along the coast provide sport for big game anglers from all over the world. The main hot-spot is dusty Malindi, where the long-established Malindi Big Game Club has been a centre for local and visiting anglers since Hemingway himself came to Africa. Many anglers stay at the aptly named 'Hemingway's Hotel' at Watamu, about 9 miles from Malindi. Hemingway's Hotel is a beautifully designed, impeccably run hotel, where the talk is of fishing and the food is of gourmet standard. This is coastal Africa at its best, where there are sands, palm trees and guaranteed sunshine, tempered only by a cooling breeze.

Malindi is a town with an ancient history of slave trading, and the Afro-Arab connection is reflected in both the architecture and the faces of its inhabitants. It is a hotchpotch town of constant movement and a host of tiny shops and bazaars, best known for the trading Arab dhows and the inland coffee plantations and lucrative cashew groves. From the front of Malindi a long and rather suspect pier or jetty projects into a shallow, muddy sea, and it is here that the local big-game boats wait offshore, their clients being rowed out to the hired vessels in a variety of neglected dinghies. Malindi may seem drab and run down, but once you are offshore the town vanishes and the sea reverts to the lovely indigo blue of the Indian Ocean.

When the sailfish run is at its height, the fish can be contacted less than half an hour out from the dock. Traditionally, this is a lure-fishing area, where the rampaging sailfish strike at fast-running surface lures. When the sailfish abound, each boat may run four or five small Kona-Head-style lures, each of which will be fitted with a different overskirt and underskirt: blue over white to imitate mackerel, green over yellow to simulate small dorado, black over pink to look like angry squid, and so on. The aim is to determine just what colour is attracting sailfish on that day, and, as soon as fish have been seen to rap or shadow a particular colour, the other lures are changed for the colour of the day. When a sailfish intercepts and takes a bait, it must be given time to take the bait properly. This means that the angler must 'drop back' to the fish. This calls for co-ordination, which comes only from experience. The moment the strike occurs, the angler must knock the reel out of gear and allow the fish to run on a free line. At this stage the line must be kept from over-running by gentle pressure of the thumb: too much thumb and the fish will drop the bait; not enough, and the reel will go into free spin and produce a bird's nest that only a sharp knife can cure. Normally, a running sailfish is allowed to take 30 or 40 yards of line before the gear lever is pushed up to strike pressure and the rod lifted to set the hook. If the angler does the job correctly, the sailfish will be soundly hooked and the battle for supremacy will start. Indian Ocean sailfish fight like all sailfish, exploding out of the water to tail-walk across the surface with a power far beyond their weight before diving to a last refuge in the deeps. There they finish the fight in a circling or zigzag motion that keeps the rod top wagging and the angler on his toes until the mate grasps the beak and leans over to place a tag and loosen the hook before releasing the fish.

One of the wonderful things about fishing the Kenya coast is the

vast variety of fish. In fact, many boats run two surface lures for sail-fish and two down-riggers with huge plug baits. The surface lures take sailfish, wahoo, kingfish and, with luck, a blue or black marlin. The deep-running plugs take yellow-fin tuna, dorado and the mighty karambizi, a huge member of the pike tribe. This last is a heavy-headed bruiser of a fish, which makes the angler pay dearly for every yard of line gained. Occasionally a big, rakish barracuda will also snatch at the plug bait. Despite its speedy appearance and fearsome reputation, the barracuda is not a great fighter but it adds interest to the day. On a good day off Malindi the catch will consist of six or eight species of hard-fighting fish, but the lovely sailfish has pride of place in any catch. Sailfish may not have the build or weight of the bull-shouldered black or blue marlin, but this lack of weight is more than compensated for by its physical beauty. It is a living fight-ing jewel of a fish, which does not know how to give up.

Fishing in Kenya usually starts at around 6 o'clock in the morning and finishes twelve hours later, when the blazing sun vanishes into the darkening Indian Ocean. With fishing over, it is time to retire to the Malindi Big Game Club or to the hotel for a shower, a drink, food and a never-ending, never-boring discussion on the day's fishing and the fishing of other seasons. The discussion may cover many species of fish, but in a sailfish area it will ultimately return to the world's great sailfish venues. Now that fly-fishing techniques are being applied to the sport of sail fishing the whole subject is set to alter course. The old days of mass killings, when dozens of fish were hung up on the dock, are almost gone. Today's anglers have the apti-tude and the tackle to take huge fish in a truly sporting manner. To tie a streamer fly and cast it to a cruising sailfish must be the ultimate in sport-fishing, and it shows an understanding and respect for sport-fishing that can have evolved only through experience of the whole range of big game fishing experiences. Today's anglers have learned from the trials and mistakes of the Zane Greys of the big game world. By modern standards their tackle was crude, heavy and not particularly efficient. Technological advances have produced rods and reels of the lightest materials, which have made it possible to catch oceanic fighters on tackle little heavier than would be used for trout. Sailfish are just the first target species. Many other fish will follow in the wake of this fly-fishing revolution.

13
BLACK MARLIN

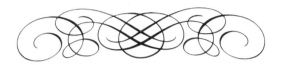

ON AVERAGE, THE black marlin (*Makaira indica*) is larger than the blue marlin, and most anglers believe that it ultimately grows larger than the largest blue marlin. Japanese long-line records, however, indicate that this is not so – and who can argue with a nation devoted to catching fish and keeping full weight and length charts of all major game fish species? To confuse matters, however, the Japanese refer to the black marlin as the white marlin, the blue marlin as the black marlin, and the prolific striped marlin as the red marlin.

Unlike the other marlin, which prefer to live and feed in deep water, the black marlin will often wander into comparatively shallow water. It is a cruiser, a fish that is constantly on the move in search of food. Most of its hunting is done by sight, and experienced black marlin anglers claim that this species has the best eyesight of all the marlin tribe. Once it has sighted a bait, it will come after it with the typical marlin aggression. To see a 1,000lb fish heading for a lure is one of the heart-stopping sights of big game fishing.

Big black marlin are normally found off the Queensland coast of Australia, the Peruvian coast of South America, parts of the Indian Ocean and occasionally off the coast of Baja California, but the world's hot-spot is the Australian town of Cairns. Here, in the comparatively short black marlin season, competition is high and the costs higher still. Black marlin fishing is a highly competitive sport that brings out the best and the worst in the moneyed world of big game fishing. Cairns boats are normally long pre-booked, attracting a clientele from all over the world. Some Americans even ship their own boats over for the season. The actor Lee Marvin was a frequent visitor to Cairns, but most of the regulars are wealthy businessmen from the USA, Japan, Germany and other industrialized countries. With the ever-present chance of boating a record-breaker, the

Australian fishing is not cheap, but it does bring you into contact with some of the world's great anglers.

During the past decade the island of Mauritius has gained quite a name for producing good-sized black marlin in consistent numbers. Like most islands in the Indian Ocean, Mauritius is something of an earthly paradise – an island of white, sandy beaches, swaying palm trees and an endless indigo blue seascape.

There was a time when most black marlin were caught on trolled natural baits, small kingfish and barracuda being the most popular. Technology moves forwards, however, and today many black marlin fall to 'plastics', man-made, acrylic and soft-head baits, loosely based on the original Kona Head lure from Hawaii and made in factories in the USA, South Africa, Britain and Australia. Each brand has its aficionados, who swear that their favourite model or make will raise more fish than any other pattern. Obviously, an angler who has confidence in his or her lures will catch more than who does not. We all have fads and fancies, of course, but I think that on its day any good lure will catch fish. An excellent all-round pattern for marlin is the tinker lure, Doorknobs, from South Africa. This broad-headed lure puts up an impressive wake which seems to induce large marlin to give chase. On a recent trip to the island of Madeira I saw a 1,000lb-plus blue marlin hit one of these lures, and I know that many big black marlin have found them irresistible, too.

Not all black marlin are monsters, and a good area to make contact with the welter-weight fish is off the coast of Kenya. Here, black marlin weighing 200–400lb are comparatively common. The fishing is not expensive, and the chances of success high. From the sea, the Kenyan coastline looks flat and green, and the beaches are mostly shielded from sight by the white surge of the tide as it breaks over the protective offshore reefs. Outside the reefs, however, the sea soon becomes deep blue as the sea bed falls away into big fish country. By American standards, Kenyan sport-fishing boats are small – cocky little 30–34ft boats, which ride the Indian Ocean swell like a custom-built seagull. Each boat carries a captain and two mates, all of whom are experts in the ways of the local fish and the best ways to catch them. These are men whose knowledge comes from experience. They are men who have been in or on the sea since before they could walk.

I can recall one bright African day when the swell was light and the fish rather few and far between. As always, we had trolled the traditional zigzag pattern to search over the grounds beneath our keel, but, apart from one fair kingfish and a small barracuda, there had been little action. As often happens during an inactive day under a hot sun, we were all dozing in the cockpit. Suddenly came the shout 'marlin', and there, weaving in our wake was that tell-tale shadow that denotes a big fish. Twice the shadow edged forwards to inspect a lure, twice it sheared away. Just when we thought it had gone for good, it was back, uncertain but definitely interested in a big, blue, soft-head lure with a green and yellow skirt. To the marlin the soft head must have looked like a small dorado. Kenyan marlin eat quantities of dorado, and we expected a strike at any second. Nothing happened. Instead, the fish simply faded away.

Both the skipper and crew thought it was a good-sized black marlin, and they decided to go back over the grounds in the hope of inducing more positive action from the vanished fish. Often retracing the path of the boat will work, and a fish that has been undecided about a bait may regret the decision and take advantage of a second opportunity. For about twenty minutes we ran lures all over the area, but to no avail. Finally, the skipper gave up, and we began to work back offshore. Within seconds the same, or a similar, marlin was on the baits. This time there was no stealth, instead the fish came roaring into the wake, inspected each bait and made its decision. There was no hesitation – it wanted the lure with dorado colours, and it hit like a freight train. In a situation like this, split seconds seem like long minutes. I can still see that final rush, the wall of white water and the heavy beak wagging over the bait. Then there was only the click of the line coming from the outrigger clip, followed by the scream of the big Shimano reel. Within seconds, the allocated angler was in the chair, rod in gimbal, fumbling desperately to snap the harness clips onto the reel lugs. Black marlin are jumpers, and this one was mad. When you look at the broad body of a big black marlin it does not seem possible that a fish that shape could possibly leap from the ocean. In action, however, the black marlin is all muscle and driving tail. This particular fish put on the whole display of aerobatics that any hooked marlin could hope to muster. It greyhounded, it tail-walked, it stood on its tail and shook its broad head, the lower jaw open, gills flaring, and always the madly dancing lure was hanging down trace of the hooks. Every motion of the head caused the lure to jump and weave, until it seemed certain that the hook would be dislodged. Few black marlin fight deep. It may be that fear of shark mutilation keeps them on the surface, but theirs is a visual battle, a sort of 'look at me and fear me' strategy that can, and does, strike fear into an angler's heart. Often they rear up close to the boat, and the frightening prospect of one jumping inboard has caused many an angler to lock up.

Fortunately, this great black opal of a fish wore itself down in a comparatively short period. Soon it was circling astern, tired but still strong. The initial show of power had been impressive, but the fish was weakening now, and, barring accidents, it was just a matter of hand work and time. Finally the leader was up for the fifth time, and this time the mate was in control. On the four previous occasions he had grasped the heavy nylon, only to have the fish rip it out of his hands. Now man was in control and the marlin knew it. Too tired to protest, it lay stiffly out from the boat transom. Only the steady rise and fall of the gills and the light in its huge eye showed it was alive. By black marlin standards it was no monster, weighing about 400lb at most. A baby by Australian standards, but a thing of wonder and beauty to the angler who had caught it, a dream catch in a once-in-a-lifetime holiday. In a week's time he would be back in a drab city in the north of England, walking to work on a wet winter morning. Inwardly, however, he would never be the same again. He would always have the smell of Africa in his nostrils and the memory of this great, dark fish wallowing gently in the trough of a light Indian Ocean swell. It was his decision to kill or release, and he chose to release. The fish was tagged, and the big hook was eased from the great mouth. Then it was gone. A dream come true, and a dream gone forever.

14
BLUE MARLIN

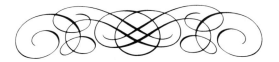

BIG BLUE MARLIN (*Makaira nigricans*) can be found round some of the world's loveliest islands – the Bahamas, Cuba, the Caymans, the Virgin Islands, Hawaii and so on – but one of the world's hot-spots is the nine-island chain of the Azores. Each island in the chain is part of the mid-Atlantic ridge. These mountains in the sea extend to form a natural barrier in the waters of the blue Atlantic. The Azores islands are naturally rich in fish of many kinds, and also provide migrating game fish with a rich natural larder, a place to stop for a while and feed up before once again vanishing back into the open ocean.

Once known as the Western or Fortunate Isles, the Azores are mountainous islands, rich in flowers, cattle and cultivated land. Each island has its own special characteristics, and each is capable of producing marlin, although only two islands contain charter fishing boats. The first, São Miguel, is a large, lovely island that is rich in spectacular lakes, thermal geysers and an ever-changing carpet of beautiful wild flowers. The second fishing point is al'Horta, on the distant island of Faial. Often known as the Isla Azul, or Blue Island, Faial's heights are covered by mile after mile of blue hydrangeas, and from the sea the island appears as a solid blue mass. Six miles away lies the island of Pico, which is dominated by a towering volcanic peak, Pico Alto, the highest mountain in Portugal at a staggering 7,712ft. To the north lies São George, whose looming cliffs can be clearly seen on all but the foggiest day.

Within the triangle created by these three islands, lie some of the best marlin fishing grounds in the world. Any Faial marlin under 500lb is reckoned to be a small fish – marlin of more than double this weight have been taken off the island. Even larger fish have been seen, hooked and finally lost. During the past decade this tiny island

has become a centre for the world's top marlin men, and few of them have left empty-handed. Almost every day's fishing in the Azores carries a story, and the following is typical of the kind of action the islands can produce.

We left Faial a little after dawn on a misty morning in late September. Across the channel the great sweep of Pico Alto dominated the scene. At one point the mountain disappeared into cloud, leaving only its notched peak standing out starkly in the light of the morning sun. I had lived on or visited the Azores for over twenty years, and yet I never ceased to marvel at the grandeur of Pico Alto, and today was no exception. Beyond the harbour entrance the skipper turned on the power to send the fishing boat streaking out into calm blue water. Our destination was the tip of an underwater mountain called the Condor bank. The Condor rises out of thousands of feet of water, but at its highest point it is still 774 feet from the surface. It is a fish-rich area, holding vast stocks of bottom-feeding fish plus huge shoals of free-swimming horse mackerel, and it is these horse mackerel that bring giant blue marlin to the area by the dozen. Only the day before I had taken a 450lb and a 600lb blue from the bank, and my partner in the boat had lost two good fish before finally saving his day by catching a monster blue weighing 780lb.

With yesterday's fish and my aching shoulders to spur me on, the two-man crew and I were determined that this, my last fishing day on the island, was going to be something special. We knew where the marlin had been thickest and, with luck, they would still be cruising over the same ground. The Azores fishing relies largely on the use of Kona-Head-style lures. Natural baits are seldom, if ever, used because they attract the big mako shark that abound in this section of the Atlantic. On this day we ran four baits: a pink Knuckle Head with a red and yellow skirt; two standard Kona Heads rigged with blue over silver skirts to simulate horse mackerel colours; and a drilled-out metal head with a green and yellow skirt, intended to look like a small dorado or dolphin fish. We started fishing the lures only when we had passed a great fire-whitened crater known as Castelo Branco (White Castle), from where it is roughly 12 miles to the Condor bank – 12 miles in which we could raise a big blue at any time. There is something fascinating about watching a string of churning, bubbling artificials working astern of a boat. On this day the sea was so calm that each lure could be clearly seen as it was towed along in our wake. For well over an hour nothing happened, except for a school of dolphins, joining us for a bow-wave-riding romp. For ten minutes these lovely mammals surged and played, before they grew bored with the never-changing speed of the moving boat.

By now we were approaching yesterday's hot-spot. Would the fish still be in the vicinity? Returning to a particular area is always something of a gamble. A shift in wind, a change in air pressure or the difference in the tide can move the bait fish, and with them will go the marlin. We need not have worried, for less than half a mile from the point where I had caught yesterday's 660-pounder, we found the fish. Not one, not a double-header, but a grand slam of strikes on all lures. Four marlin on at one time is something I had never heard of in all my years of fishing, and here I was, the only angler on the boat, and four big fish up and jumping. Grabbing the left rigger rod, I saw my line was actually across the mouth of a fish hooked on the flat-line bait. Fortunately this fish jumped itself off, and my line fell out of its mouth. By this time, the other fish had jumped free, and I was left to put some pressure on my fish, which was fully intent on greyhounding over the horizon. Marlin that start the fight on the surface seldom sustain a serious crash dive. In Hemingway's classic *The Old Man and the Sea* the old fisherman prayed for his fish to fight on top. 'That way,' he said, 'the fish would fill the air sacs along its back.' I believe there is an element of truth in this idea.

I was fishing 80lb-class tackle and had every confidence in boating this fish, which looked as if it weighed more than 400lb. For a while the marlin vented its anger on the dangling lure. Time and again it stood on its tail and shook its great head and long beak. Then it gave up this show of surface violence and dived deep. At this stage I knew it was mine, and I somehow sensed that it was weakening. When it took line, it stopped short of its earlier runs, giving line grudgingly but giving it none the less. It took forty-five minutes from hook-up to capitulation. In the water the fish looked around 450lb, and, although it might have been a little more, it certainly was not any less. When the mate took the leader, the fish hardly moved, and, even when it was pulled in close and held by the bill, it barely wagged its lovely tail. With the hooks out we gently turned the magnificent creature loose. For a moment or two it did not seem to realize, or perhaps care, that it was free. Then it came to, steadied itself and sped off into the dark blue depths. Long may it live as a free spirit, one of nature's wonders that only the lucky among us have ever seen.

By the standards of the Azores this fish was small, and what we wanted now was its mother or, better still, its grandmother. Twice in the next hour good-sized fish came up to look over the lures, but on both occasions the fish ran the lure, then shied away. Then came thirty minutes without a sighting, but, just when it looked as if the marlin had gone, the water opened and a huge fish slammed into the bait. On the first pass it missed the lure completely. This sent it berserk. Throwing caution to the wind, it went for the Kona Head with a vengeance, and I shall never forget the sight of the raging demon of a fish as it accelerated through the surface film. When it sucked in the bait, every inch of the fish was bristling, the blue lights on its body cells lit up the water for yards around, making this the most spectacular marlin attack I have ever been privileged to witness.

Hooking up was a formality, but what happened next was not. Once it was hooked, I expected the big blue to charge off across the surface. Instead, it stood on its tail only yards from the boat and gave a display of strength and temper that no other fish in the world could begin to match. At close range, its great head seemed to wag in slow motion, while its tail beat the water to flying foam. Twice it went down, only to rear up again in more or less the same position. When this ploy failed to dislodge the hook and flailing bait, it took off on a long, magnificent, tail-waving run. The first run must have stripped over 150 yards from the wildly protesting reel before the fish changed tactics and dived. In less than five minutes it was back on the surface, standing on its tail and again flailing its huge body from side to side. It is amazing how such a huge fish can sustain this position. The strength and power generated by the great scythe of the tail are obviously enormous. For my part I was happy to let it perform. Every tail wag took a little of its energy, and, when it finally vanished into the depths, I knew we were in the last but most critical stage of the battle. This was when the hard work started. Punishment was going to be handed out on both sides, and I braced myself for the clash. Thirty minutes of gain and lose, and I had the fish in sight. But only for a while. Then it was stalemate, with the monster lying ten yards off the stern, refusing to give an inch of ground. These last stages of a big-fish battle are always the most exhausting. Both combatants are tired, and the vastly superior weight of the fish takes its toll of the angler. At this stage, the fun was gone from the fight. Inch by precious inch, I gained line, until, with a sudden and welcome click, the trace swivel hit the top ring. The mate grabbed the trace, and I turned the lever drag back a notch in

case the fish came alive and crash dived. Fortunately, the fish was exhausted, and even when gaffed it barely moved its tail. Only the slow pumping of the gill plates showed it was still alive. Late that night it weighed in at 856lb – my best-ever blue marlin and at that time a new European record. Like all giant blue marlin, my fish was a female. The males seldom reach weights of much more than 300lb, and there is a belief that marlin change sex when they reach a certain weight.

The Azores and Madeira are exceptions to the general laws of marlin fishing in that they produce a seemingly endless stream of big fish on an almost daily basis. Anglers from most of the recognized marlin ports in the world are lucky if they see a marlin on every eight or ten trips, and big marlin occur only once or twice in a year's fishing. The most important thing for the angler to remember is that any marlin, irrespective of its size, is a special fish, and the only luck in marlin fishing is in the size of the fish you catch.

15
BROADBILL
SWORDFISH

LIKE THE BLUE marlin, the broadbill swordfish (*Xiphias gladius*) is found around the world. Unlike the blue marlin, which is rarely seen until it races in to strike a lure, the broadbill is often an obvious fish, basking away the hot hours on the surface of the sea, a characteristic that for many years made it a target fish for specially designed harpooning boats. What the anglers in the early years of the century failed to realize, however, was that a basking swordfish was very rarely a feeding swordfish. From the turn of the century right up to the 1960s it was the custom to bait and tease these basking monsters in the hope that one would wake up and snatch at a bait or lure. This rarely happened, and nine out of ten boated swordfish were, in fact, foul-hooked, usually in the head or shoulders and usually because the exasperated skipper had deliberately dragged the bait across the back of the sleeping fish. A few were taken fair and square by using live baits, but even then catches were low. What these anglers and skippers missed was that the swordfish is a night or early morning hunter, searching for food at depths below 1,200 or 1,800 ft. These fish have been photographed at depths of over 2,000ft. One bad-tempered individual actually attacked the Woods Hole Institute submersible at this depth, getting its bill jammed in the process.

Since the late 1970s the technique of fishing for swordfish has changed, and what was once considered a rare catch has become just another billfish. To reach this point, the whole lore of sword fishing was picked apart and compared with reports from commercial fishermen. The other spectacular catches produced by deep-set, long lines made it obvious that surface-fishing was out and deep baiting was in. The revolution started off Florida and quickly spread around the world. Lures and natural fish baits were discarded in favour of whole natural squid, rigged with a chemical light-stick insert. The combination of the fresh-smelling squid and the green glow of the activated light-stick proved a deadly combination. Anglers who would normally only fish in daylight hours became night birds, and, as they did so, swordfish catches increased dramatically. Target areas were the deep, underwater canyons and the edges of deep banks. This was a highly productive waiting game, akin in many ways to standard shark fishing procedures. The only difference was that a swordfish boat did not carry or use chum or rubby-dubby. Usually each boat fished three or more baits at staggered depths, the shallowest bait being set at 100ft with the other two being in 100ft increments. Once a swordfish was hooked, caught or lost, the other baits were re-set to the known taking depths on that particular night.

Since those experimental Florida night trips, this technique has become the recognized method for taking swordfish throughout the sport-fishing world. Interestingly, however, long before the excepted American big game experts began to think seriously about deep fishing for broadbill, a similar rod-and-line industry was established on the Portuguese mainland, south of Lisbon. Here, at the tiny village of Sezimbra, local hotelier José Braz had established both a hotel and a reputation for putting his clientele on to some hot swordfishing. As early as the 1940s Dr Arsenio Cordeiro had started catching swordfish in the area, and this led José Braz to build the Hotel Espedarte (Swordfish Hotel) and to develop the magnificent fishing into a localized tourist industry.

Lovely Sezimbra lies at the foot of a rocky escarpment on the sheltered side of a mighty headland called Cabo Espichel (Cape Especial). The village has been established since the tenth century and at one time was under Moorish domination. When Braz built the Hotel Espedarte, Sezimbra had yet to be discovered by the rest of Europe. Only anglers and many Lisbon residents came to the village – one group to catch fish, the other to eat them. Even today, the bars and restaurants of Sezimbra are still the place to go to eat grilled sardines washed down with bottles of cold Vinho Verde, the white wine of Portugal.

The sword fishing techniques used in Sezimbra were good but brutal on the angler. Each day, an hour or two before daybreak, prospective anglers left the hotel to take a seat on an old but reliable fishing boat. Later, as the lovely dawn light lifted the limited visibility of night, it was possible to see a cluster of small boats huddled together on an apparently featureless blue sea. Each angler, his rod,

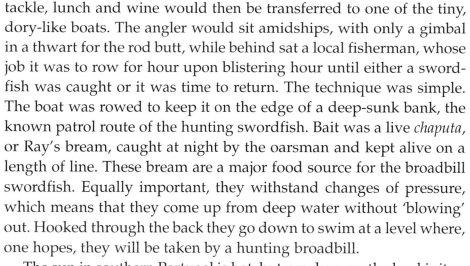

tackle, lunch and wine would then be transferred to one of the tiny, dory-like boats. The angler would sit amidships, with only a gimbal in a thwart for the rod butt, while behind sat a local fisherman, whose job it was to row for hour upon blistering hour until either a swordfish was caught or it was time to return. The technique was simple. The boat was rowed to keep it on the edge of a deep-sunk bank, the known patrol route of the hunting swordfish. Bait was a live *chaputa*, or Ray's bream, caught at night by the oarsman and kept alive on a length of line. These bream are a major food source for the broadbill swordfish. Equally important, they withstand changes of pressure, which means that they come up from deep water without 'blowing' out. Hooked through the back they go down to swim at a level where, one hopes, they will be taken by a hunting broadbill.

The sun in southern Portugal is hot, but nowhere on the land is it as hot as on the ocean. Yet despite the heat and the lack of action, the oarsman will keep up a steady, measured stroke. The tiny boat is going nowhere, but it must be kept from drifting off the edge of the deep-sunk bank. Scattered down the unseen line of the bank float a dozen similar boats, the tiny 12ft cockleshells that are painted in the bright colours that Portuguese fisherman love so well. Each little boat carries its crew of two – the oarsman, in his brightly checked fisherman's shirt and cap or beret, and the angler, who is better dressed and who holds the great rod and reel. The anglers are from some distant European city, and just beginning to realize a dream that is more uncomfortable and hot than could ever be imagined. The thwart of these little boats is an uncomfortable place for a man used to a car or swivel chair, and yet beneath the discomfort lies the hope that a swordfish will slash at the free-swimming bait. For some it never happens, but for the fortunate few comes the strike that, once felt, can never be forgotten.

My own particular moment of truth came after four days of fishing. Only one broadbill had been caught during that period, and the dory seat was as uncomfortable as ever. My oarsman spoke no English, and I spoke no Portuguese – anyway, it is not possible to hold a conversation with someone sitting behind you. On that day I had been fishing from 5 o'clock in the morning, and it was now well past noon. The heat was building up, and I was beginning to question the sanity of the whole expedition. Then the fish struck the bait. One second nothing, the next the rod slammed down as, somewhere far below, a broadbill slashed at the bait with its short, flat beak. Steeped in the theory of sword fishing, I threw the reel out of gear to let the bait drop naturally through the deep dark water. Broadbills slap a bait to kill or stun it, and then they watch it free fall for a few seconds before turning to intercept and swallow it. What the angler has to do is simulate that falling away motion of the bait fish. I suppose I let 30–40ft of line trickle off the slowly turning reel spool before feeling the fish gently take the bait. I expected a savageness, a display of aggression, but instead I felt a strange quivering vibration on the line. This quickly turned to a slow insistent pulling, and I could sense the fish swallowing the big bait. Slowly, but with steadily increasing persistence, the fish began to take line. As I put the reel into gear, I knew that I was going to find out what fighting a swordfish was like from a small boat. There was no fighting chair – just a plain brass gimbal and a shoulder harness to see me through. Striking was hardly necessary. When the fish felt the drag of the big rod and the rasp of heavy trace on its side, it went wild. From a slow forwards motion, it lunged for the sea bed in an undersea explosion of action. Where once we had been bobbing serenely on blue water, the little boat was being dragged stern first across the surface. Fortunately the fish was taking line as well, which gave me time to settle on the thwart and to shrug my harness into a comfortable position.

Several times during the following two hours we passed other rowing boats, whose occupants waved and showed encouragement. What was said and in what language I cannot say. I could see and hear little through a haze of physical and mental activity. My hands were full, and my brain was working overtime. Gradually the fish began to weaken. It still swam deep, but some of the fire was gone, and nothing goads an angler on more than sensing a weakness in the opponent. As the fish lost strength, I seemed to gain from its weakness. Now the old fishing boat was standing by, its crew lining the rails with the big swordfish gaff. Finally it was in sight, an indistinct brown shape, far down in the clear water. I was able to force it up gradually, until finally it surfaced. A great leathery brown, prehistoric-looking fish with huge eyes, a gaping mouth and a feebly wagging bill. I could hardly believe my luck – I was about to join the then few anglers who had caught a broadbill. Slowly the fishing boat eased closer, the gaffs reached down and the hook was pulled out. Instantly, the fish was on its way. Back to the blackness of deep water. I swore then I would never fish or even visit lovely Sezimbra again, and I never have. The swordfish are now long absent from those banks of Portugal, swept away by lines of foreign long-line boats, and fish that were once only eaten locally now bring a high price in the fish markets of the world. Sezimbra is just one other casualty of over-fishing.

16
SHARK

EW OF THE many species of shark rate as true big game fish. Most sharks are slow, sluggish creatures that are disinclined to show any turn of speed when they are hooked. There are, of course, exceptions to every rule, and in the shark world this exception is the mighty mako shark. Once described as 'blue dynamite', the mako is capable of putting on a display of aerobatics that not even marlin can equal. Commercial fisherman from South America call the mako *albacora con dientes* – swordfish with teeth – but no swordfish can hope to out-jump a fighting mako. There are two types of mako, the short-fin mako (*Isurus oxyrinchus*) and the long-fin mako (*I. pancus*), but the short-fin species is the one most likely to be caught by anglers. The long-fin mako tends to be a nocturnal feeder, with a liking for deep water. The short-fin mako prefers daylight feeding and hunts close to the surface. Every inch oceanic sharks, mako rarely occur in shallow water. In the volcanic islands of the Atlantic they may be caught closer to land, but only in areas where the seabed plunges to depths in excess of 600 ft.

Mako are fast-moving, active hunters, which feed for the most part on rapidly moving species. Tuna, bonito and bluefish are their natural prey, but they also attack and kill broadbill swordfish, and a big mako will often show a series of body scars from encounters with large swordfish. Mako are fast movers, and they are capable of sustaining high speeds for quite long periods. To achieve this speed, their body temperatures are normally 7–10 degrees higher than the surrounding water. Unlike most sharks, which tend to travel in loose packs, the mako is normally a loner, although very small mako, of 40 to 60lb, may travel in small gangs. Once they reach a weight of around 100lb the fish revert to type and prefer a solitary existence. Female mako reach maximum weights of 1,200 to 1,300lb. The males

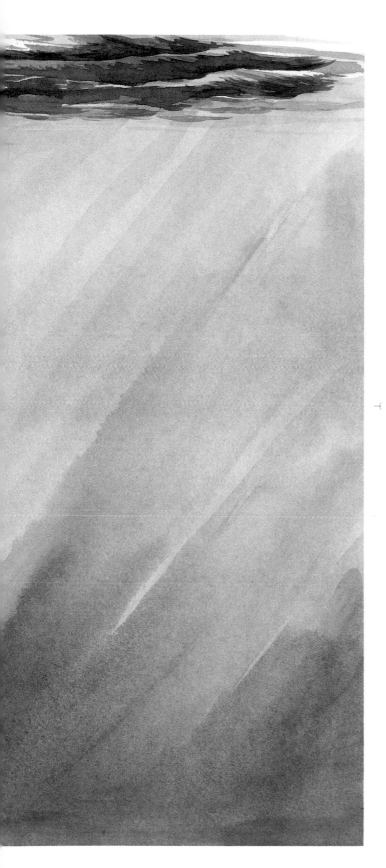

tend to be smaller. Anglers often see a mako before it attempts to take a bait, because, for some reason, these aggressive sharks like to inspect boats at close quarters. When a mako is seen, its jaws are usually half-open, giving a clear view of its long, snaggy teeth. A distinctly pretty fish, the mako has a steel-blue back and snowy white underparts.

The name mako comes from the Maori word for the species, and New Zealand is one of the great places to fish for the shark and stand a fair chance of catching them on a regular basis. The Azores are another mako hot-spot, where these fish can be captured in reasonable quantities, but elsewhere it is difficult to set out deliberately to catch one of these magnificent sharks. Instead, it is better to set out for a day's general fishing and to hope that a mako drifts into the chum line. Like all sharks, mako have a highly developed sense of smell, and they can be easily attracted by a constant stream of minced fish and fish oil. Once stimulated, they will take a dead fish, although they much prefer live bait, and large live mackerel or horse mackerel make first-class baits for mako. When a dead bait is used, it should be an oily fleshed fish – bonito or small black-fin tuna are near perfect.

Despite its speed and ferocity, the mako can be a delicate feeder. A typical take on drift-fished baits may just make the reel click a couple of times. Once this happens, the reel should be put into free spool and the rod tip lowered. This will stop the fish from feeling any major resistance as it mouths at the bait. Once the shark becomes confident it will move off with the bait across its jaws, and, during this stage, line should be given freely. Normally, the mako will take 20–30 yards of line, then stop to turn and swallow the bait. The strike should be made as it begins to move off for the second time. Then it is time to look out. Mako do not take kindly to a hook being driven solidly into their jaws. Their reaction is sudden and invariably savage. All gentleness is forgotten as the fish comes out of the water like a guided missile. Seeing one of these magnificent sharks explode from the sea is one of the greatest sights a big game angler can experience. Some people speak of mako going up 30ft in the air, and, although this is probably an exaggeration, heights of 15ft or more are definitely attained. To make the jump even more impressive, the fish normally turns over at the top of the jump to crash back into water in a welter of high-flying spray. Once the fish gives up jumping, it normally turns on the speed and tears away at high speed. The angler must be prepared for this rush, otherwise the line will break. An overtight drag invariably means the line will snap, but too light a drag means that the fish may empty the reel spool. Once the first major run is over, the mako has to be worked hard. Given a chance to rest, the fish will regain its strength in minutes.

Mako shark are highly active and will chase and take trolled artificial lures. All-black Kona Head lures seem to be highly attractive to a hungry mako shark, and they normally hit the lure so hard that they hook themselves in the process. The drawback to lure-fishing is that the impact of fish and bait is so great that the lure is destroyed in the process. These days anglers prefer to use stand-up rods for most shark-fishing expeditions, and, although taking a large mako without the aid of a fighting chair may sound like hard work, the short, powerful rods, combined with a correctly used stand-up harness and butt pad, can quickly wear down the largest mako shark. Care must be taken to play out a mako completely before attempting to boat it. More than one 'green' mako has actually jumped into a boat, causing considerable damage to both the boat and the angler.

Compared to the racy mako, its near relative, the great white shark, relies on bulk rather than speed. The shark (*Carcharodon carcharias*) was immortalized in the film *Jaws*, which accurately portrayed the white shark's penchant for raiding shallow, inshore areas. The largest known carnivorous fish, white sharks, which are thought to reach lengths of 30ft, can be found in all but the coldest of the world's oceans. They have a fearsome and well-founded reputation for attacks on human beings, and there are many well-documented attacks on skin divers clad in dark-coloured rubber suits. White sharks show a liking for sea lion meat, and it could be that the rubber-clad diver, complete with flipper-like fins, is mistaken for an adult sea lion.

White shark show a distinct preference for cool water, and south Australia, South Africa, northern California and the eastern end of Long Island, New York, are all white shark strongholds. The Atlantic islands of Madeira and the Azores group also attract the usually unwanted attentions of cruising white shark. Like the mako, the white is a lone wanderer, but in a food-rich area small groups may gather to give an illusion of a pack of white sharks. Unlike the mako, which prefers to catch its food alive, the white shark will also become a scavenger. In the days when active whale factories operated in Madeira and the Azores, the constant seepage of blood and rotting meat would quickly draw white sharks inshore, and huge specimens were regularly harpooned near to these whaling stations.

The largest game fish yet taken on rod and line was a 2,664lb monster, which was caught in Australian waters by the late Alfred Dean, although fish of over 3,000lb have been harpooned. Since the film *Jaws* was released, white shark stocks have decreased rapidly, largely because of the high demand for teeth and complete jaws. Even so, white shark fishing is still a viable sport. Catching such a shark requires the heaviest of sport fishing tackle, and the sheer bulk of a fighting great white calls for every ounce of power the angler can apply. Under the rules of the IGFA, this means 130lb test tackle. Baits range from whole tuna to huge chunks of horse flesh, and the hook is usually attached to ultra-heavy wire or is brazed to a length of chain. Once hooked, a great white does not attempt to jump. Instead, it relies on its great strength and gigantic tail. Individual fish have been fought for over twenty-four hours and have still managed to break away. Others sharks have attacked the boat so persistently that the reluctant angler has been forced to cut the rampaging monster adrift. Those that have been brought to the gaff have invariably fought themselves and the angler to a standstill.

Strangely, the odd monster has been deliberately taken on ultra-light line. No noticeable pressure can be applied with a 6, 10, or 12lb b.s. line, and instead the fish has to be followed and hammered for hours until it finally succumbs to nervous exhaustion – hardly a sporting way to catch the greatest of fighting sharks.

There is a theory that, at a certain stage in its growth, the white shark forsakes its normal habitat and vanishes for ever into the vast depths. Certainly, there is plenty of evidence to indicate that gigantic white sharks have been sighted from time to time. Fish said to be 70 or 90ft long have been recorded, and, if this is indeed the case, our giant great whites are little more than the babies of the tribe.

In today's world of diminishing catches and increasing angling costs, not all of the true big game fish are easily accessible to many anglers. The high cost of a black marlin expedition, for example, now means that only the really wealthy can indulge themselves with this kind of fishing. This has led anglers to turn to other species for good but not expensive sport, and one of the species that has come in for close scrutiny is the blue shark (*Prionace glauca*), a long, lean shark that grows to a weight of over 450lb. Blue sharks are a plentiful species, which offer the angler good sport at reasonable cost.

Blue sharks are comparatively common around Britain during the summer months. Occasionally the fish seem to decline in numbers, only to re-establish themselves after a few lean years. Despite fluctuating catches there is a long-established shark club in Britain, with headquarters in Looe, Cornwall. American anglers have a similar blue shark fishery off Montauk, Long Island, a fishery that has become increasingly popular in recent years. Most rod-caught blue sharks tend to weigh no more than around 100 or 150lb, but there are places in the world where the blue sharks run big, very big and plentiful. One such hot-spot lies between the Atlantic islands of Madeira and Porto Santo. Both islands are of volcanic origin, and both are surrounded by very deep water. I was recently fortunate to lead a fishing expedition to this area, and naturally big blue sharks were one of the major target species.

Atlantic blue sharks are very visible fish. Much of their lives are spent on, or close to, the surface of the water, and they show immense curiosity about anything that floats. Totally unafraid, they will readily approach stationary boats, almost as if they associate boats with food. On this particular trip, the shark hunt was held over until the last day, and what a day it turned out to be. As we left the north coast of Madeira and headed towards Porto Santo, the sea was flat and a deep indigo blue. Close inshore we passed numerous turtles and a small school of porpoise. Then, 5–6 miles offshore, we started to see cruising sharks. At first it was just the odd fin we saw, but this soon changed to multiple sightings, and it was obvious that we had struck an area thick with sharks. Most of the fish were big, lazy blue sharks, but several hefty hammerheads were also in evidence. Past experience shows that the cautious hammerheads were usually beaten to the bait by the even more hungry, often aggressive, blue sharks.

With plenty of fish in sight, the boat was stopped and the tackle made ready. Within seconds the large blues appeared within yards of the boat, and, to encourage them to feed, a perforated plastic container half-filled with minced fish was hung over the side. This is standard procedure on all shark boats, the theory being that a constant trickle of bait particles seeps out of the container and automatically sets up a small lane, which attracts the shark. Unfortunately, one big blue had obviously not read the rules. It got a scent of the bait and simply crunched the bucket into tiny pieces. This released the mushy contents, and the sharks moved in. We had plenty of bonito aboard as bait, and we cut this into fillets, making a rich, oily bait that proved irresistible to the patrolling shark.

The first fish to be hooked was over 300lb. What small blues seem to lack in speed and stamina, these big mid-Atlantic blues more than make up for, and this one was no exception. The second the hook was set, and as it felt the drag of rod and line, the shark switched to high gear and dived at speed for the sanctuary of deep water. On 30lb-class tackle this first plunging run was impressive. Within seconds, over 200 yards of line had been ripped off the protesting reel spool, and the fish was still moving away. For the next thirty minutes the battle was evenly poised, but finally the fish began to give ground. Even then it was no pushover and had to be handled with care. Then it was over, and as the mate grasped the heavy nylon rubbing leader the fish was in clear view. From its broad head to the tip of its immaculate tail, the shark looked every inch a fighter. The long, lean body, huge pectoral fins and clean lines made it an object of beauty, and, to add to its appearance, its beautiful blue back and clean white belly enhanced the near-perfect shape of its body. It was not a fish to be killed or even brought into the boat. Instead, it was a fish to tag and release, a fish that might wander the oceans for months or even years before it would be re-caught and the tag removed and returned. Of all the world's sharks, the blue is one of the greatest wonders, often covering thousands of miles of ocean before being recaptured elsewhere in the world.

With one good fish and many more in sight, it was not long before three anglers were hooked up and fighting their own desperate battles to control 12 or 13ft of heavy muscle. And so it went on: hook up, play out, tag and release. Some of the fish were true monsters: sharks weighing up to an estimated 450lb and every one a male. We did not see or catch a single female, which was a pity, because the females allegedly grow much larger than the males, which might mean that they reach a weight in excess of 600lb. The day passed in constant action as the tagging return forms started to build up, then, as if in climax, one of the party hooked a big hammerhead. This fish tried everything it could to break free and finally came to the boat an hour and ten minutes from hook-up time. Golden-brown in colour, the hammerhead looked ungainly against the neatness of the blue sharks, but even so it was a magnificent fish weighing an estimated 500lb. Like all the blues, it was tagged and released, swimming strongly away, apparently none the worse for its exertions. Now it was time to count the release forms and tot up the estimated overall weight of the catch. We knew we had had a good day, but what we did not realize was that we had taken twenty-four blue sharks in addition to the big hammerhead. Only two of the blue sharks were thought to have weighed under 300lb; the remainder were thought to have weighed between 300 and 450lb. These, together with the lone hammerhead, added up to a staggering catch weight of around 5 tons, a weight that is thought to be the largest single day's catch of blue sharks on record.

In European and American waters the porbeagle shark (*Lamna nasus*) is almost as popular as the blue shark as a game fish, although unfortunately, the porbeagle is not as widespread in distribution as the blue shark. Normally a cold-water species, the porbeagle is very much a pack fish, unlike the blues, which are loners, gathering in groups only in food-rich areas. Porbeagles hunt from surface to sea bed, and they will take just about anything edible that comes their way. The porbeagle packs often take up semi-permanent residence in areas that are subject to strong tidal flows, which form rips and over-falls. Such places are often frequented by mackerel shoals, and these bait fish are soon disorientated by the rush of conflicting tide flows, making them easy prey for the sleek, hard-hitting porbeagle packs.

A full-grown porbeagle shark can reach a weight of around 500lb, but most rod-caught fish weigh in at between 120 to 240lb. Any porbeagle over 250lb is classed as a good catch. Porbeagle sharks will occasionally take trolled natural or artificial lures, but for the most part they prefer live or dead fish, presented from surface level down to around 60ft. Most keen porbeagle anglers fish from drifting boats, using some form of pungent fish flesh, fish oil and bran mix to attract and hold the shark's attention. Very much a summer and early autumn pastime, porbeagling is a pleasant and often highly productive form of fishing. There is nothing nicer on a fine day than to sit in a quietly drifting boat, watching three or four partially inflated balloon floats bobbing gently over the surface. Sometimes porbeagles, like blue sharks, are very obvious fish, as they cruise rapidly around or under the boat, snuffling at the oddments of oil-soaked fish flesh dribbling out of the rubby-dubby container. At other times, mostly with large fish, there are no visual warnings. One minute nothing; the next second a screaming reel and rapidly disappearing balloon floats are the first indications that a fish is in the area. These surprise takes set the heart pounding and the adrenalin flowing.

Once hooked, a good-sized porbeagle can give a good account of itself. The fish may look like little barrels when measured against the lithe body of a good-sized blue shark, but never underestimate the strength packed into that portly frame. The porbeagle is a scrapper, and it is more than capable of putting any angler through his paces. Like the blue shark, the porbeagle never attempts to jump. Instead, it prefers to get its head down and try for the blackness of deep water. That first plunging run is the critical factor in porbeagle fishing. If you can control that first burst of speed, the fish should ultimately be yours.

Fortunately, the days are gone when anglers automatically killed each shark they took. Today, shark fishers are conservation-minded, and the fish are caught, played out and cheerfully released, in the hope that they will live on and breed to sustain future generations of keen anglers.

17
SOUTH AMERICAN DORADO

ALTHOUGH FOUR species of dorado are found in the rivers of South America, it is only the largest (*Salminus maximus*) that of interest to the serious angler. The dorado is in fact a member of the primitive characin family, to which the African tiger fish belongs. *S. maximus* is the largest representative of this family in South America, and it is surpassed in size only by the goliath tiger fish of the Congo Basin. Once common in many South American rivers, the dorado is now seriously fished for only in the rivers of Paraguay and Argentina and in selected waters in Brazil, and the season effectively starts in late October and finishes during the early part of May.

TED ANGLER P.95#21

The dorado, sometimes called the golden salmon of the rivers, is a beautiful fish. Its overall colour is a soft, yet brilliant, gold. The scales are large and of a uniform colour, although some fish have a series of slightly darker scales running along the body creating a subtle stripe. The broad yet fine fins are bright red. The exception is the tail, which has a black horizontal bar through its centre. From this bar the fins turn gold with a marginal scarlet band.

Dorados are a fast-water species, although they will occasionally take up temporary residence by bankside lily pads or among the branches of fallen trees. In many ways this habit is similar to the African tiger fish, and both species are probably aware that small fish are found around weedbeds or other sub-surface obstructions. If this is the case, the dorado simply uses the natural cover as a well-stocked

larder, because for most of their lives these fish live out in the main current, where they seem to revel in fast, well-aerated water.

Dorado fishing first enjoyed a heyday during the 1920s and 1930s, when anglers travelled for weeks, first on liners and then by tramp river steamers, to reach the interior rivers noted for the quality of their dorado fishing. During that period several books devoted to the dorado were published. One was by that noted angler J.W. Hills, who gives a lot of detailed information on the fish itself and the type of tackle needed. Hills also includes some interesting anecdotes, including one tale of a ruined expedition. He had apparently travelled for six weeks to reach a remote section of river, and on arrival he found the dorado season was in full swing. The river pools were teeming with big fish, and he could hardly wait to start fishing. On his very first cast, he hooked a big fish, which promptly snapped the line and departed. Thinking his line must have passed over a sharp rock, he accepted the loss and tied on a new lure. The next cast was a repeat of the first – a big fish hooked, only to be lost in seconds. This time he decided to test the line, and to his horror it parted at a fraction of its stated test strength. He tried again, and the same thing occurred. The line, the only one he had with him, was rotten throughout its entire length, and his nearest tackle shop was six weeks' travel away. So that was the end of the expedition. One assumes that he never again ventured into dorado country without spare lines.

Hills was writing at a time when South America was full of British and American engineers, surveyors and railway experts. Many of these men were keen anglers, and the golden dorado was a natural substitute for the native fish of their home rivers. In consequence, a specialist dorado club was formed whose members were accepted by invitation only. Tackle came from Ambercrombie & Fitch in New York or from the House of Hardy in London. Special rods were built, and the Hardy Silex reel was thought to be the ultimate spinning or bait fishing reel. During the mid- to late 1930s dorado fishing was at its zenith. Then, with the very immediate threat of war in Europe, the sport peaked and the dorado club seemed to vanish. The only tangible reminder of the time when the golden salmon of South America was king were a few articles in back issues of magazines and the few books written during the sport's great age.

Little more was heard about the dorado for the next forty years. One or two Americans made the journey south and caught fish, and each wrote in glowing terms of the fighting ability of the average dorado. A few pictures appeared, but the fish did not seem to catch the attention of most anglers. Travel was difficult, the rivers inacessible, and the terrain inhospitable. In addition, the threat of various jungle diseases made the prospect of a dorado expedition far from attractive. This situation lasted until the early 1980s, by which time South America had been tamed. Flights to all major cities were readily available, and the road, rail and river systems had so improved that once remote areas were within relatively easy reach. This encouraged a few entrepreneurs to look at the possibility of starting dorado fishing lodges at strategic places on the better rivers, and, despite initial setbacks, the permission and finance were obtained and the lodges began to spring up. The dorado were still there in quantity. They fought as hard if not harder on lightweight modern tackle, and for the first time anglers were showing interest.

At first it was mostly American anglers who took advantage of this re-born fishing, but soon the news spread, and anglers began to travel from all over the world. The travel involved and currency problems mean that dorado fishing is still an expensive sport, but nevertheless increasing numbers of anglers are booking into the lodges. Dorado fishing is back on the map.

Basically dorado can be caught in three ways. The small fish, which weigh 1–3lb, can be caught on fly rods and bright lure-type flies. This is fun-fishing, for little more than a 9ft fly rod, number 8 line and a tiny wire tippet on the cast are required. The wire is necessary because the dorado are apt to chop through plain nylon in seconds. The bigger fish are taken on heavy spinning tackle, using elongated single-hook spoons or large plugs, although these fish will also take live baits. For sheer sport, the spinning technique is probably the best way to catch large dorado. Most of the fishing is done from boats because the better fish come from deep dark pools or scours. Dorado seem to like a hard flow of water, but they will also take up station on the edge of the current, and a typical stronghold is at a point where rocks or other solid obstructions deflect the water flow. This creates an area of semi-slack water, and the dorado lurk in this, ready to shoot out into the current to intercept small fish or other food.

Like their near relative, the African tiger fish, dorado like a large lure. Although they will strike at tiny spinners, the best results are achieved with 3in wobbling spoons, and copper or gold spoons seem more attractive than silver lures. Before use, the factory-fitted treble hook should be changed for a large, well-sharpened single hook in order to give an increased hooking per strike ratio. When a dorado closes its jaw on a treble hook, its lips lock on the outside wires of the hook. The angler feels a good strike, lifts the rod and feels the fish for a second or two. Then the fish opens its mouth and is gone. The single hook is never infallible, and a certain percentage of fish will 'fall off'. However, a greater percentage will be firmly hooked.

As with the tiger fish, a hooked dorado is a demon, a fighting machine that never calls for quarter. When it is hooked, it will normally indulge in a series of spirited jumps. At the top of each leap, it will shake its head in a desperate attempt to shake free from the dangling spinner. When these aerobatics fail, the fish will settle down and make a number of long powerful runs. Finally, as its strength begins to go, the fish will give line grudgingly. Often, at the last second, it will attempt to jump again. On a short line, these can be dangerous tactics, and the line may go under strain. The fish may jump and fall back on the taut line, or the lure may simply lever itself free. This can be extremely dangerous, for suddenly released, a big spoon or plug-type bait will come back at the angler like a bullet. If the spinner hits the angler it could cause serious injury, which is bad enough during normal fishing, but on some lonely jungle river the results could be horrendous.

Most dorado weigh 8–12lb, but very much larger fish exist, so it pays to slightly over-estimate in the choice of tackle. Lines in the 12–18lb range may not cast as easily as light lines, but when an extra large fish turns up, the extra strength of the heavy line will be the deciding factor in the ensuing battle.

Dorado fishing is opening up in a big way, and for the angler who has been through the bonefish, the permit, the black bass and the tarpon, the high-jumping dorado is the perfect next choice. The South American dorado is big, bold and beautiful, and it is a fish that attracts serious attention. Whenever knowledgeable anglers gather, a man who has first-hand experience of the dorado will find himself a welcome guest.

18
SALTWATER
FLY-FISHING

T HE DEVELOPMENT of specialist tackle combined with the naturally inquiring and adventurous mind of the modern angler have meant that increasing numbers of saltwater anglers are turning to fly-casting for inshore and offshore species. The practice started the USA, with anglers like Lefty Kreh and Lee Wulff writing of their exploits with bonefish, barracuda, permit and red drum. At first most saltwater fly-casting occurred near the Florida and Bahama flats. The catches were good, the sporting quality of the fish

was excellent, and the novelty of taking good fish on lightweight fly tackle was appealing. It was not, however, until someone started fly-casting for monster tarpon that the angling public began to take serious notice. Anglers are, at best, a conservative bunch, content to stand back while a few pioneers do the real spadework, but then came the news that tarpon weighing up to and over 100lb could be taken on fly tackle. Admittedly, the fly was no imitation of a natural insect. Instead, 5–7in lures were being created to represent small fish. No matter – the principle was the same and the fly-cum-lure was cast fly-style to sighted fish.

In the early days there were no custom-built saltwater fly rods or reels. The early saltwater fly-casters had to use existing tackle or make up their own rods from other blanks. Lefty Kreh admits that one of the best saltwater fly rods he ever owned was made up from a blank designed for a spinning rod. He once remarked: 'It was hell to cast with, but once hooked up, it had all the power in the world.' Naturally, as interest in the subject grew, more and more knowledgeable fly men began to experiment with this style of fishing, and true saltwater fly rods soon came on the market. Naturally, mistakes were made, and more than one expert was left with the shattered remnants of a cherished rod. It is this sort of experience, that leads to the development of near-perfect tackle, however, and, although those pioneers may have had more than their fair share of breakages and lost fish, each mishap helped to identify a fault. One by one, the faults were ironed out, until, today, many rod-building companies produce saltwater fly rods in a wide range of lengths and line-casting weights.

The same process applied to fly reels. Existing patterns, even of salmon-taking size, were found severely wanting for saltwater work. They were either too small to hold enough backing line or to flimsy to stand up to big fish. Even when a suitable reel was found, it was normally quickly destroyed by sand particles, or by the corrosive action of saltwater. Probably the only exception was the comparatively cheap Pfleuger Medalist reel, a rugged, no frills, 4in fly reel, which held lots of backing and stood up to the rigours of use in saltwater. The drawback to the Medalist was that it had no rim control, which meant that it was impossible to apply additional finger pressure. The early saltwater fly-casters quickly overcame this problem by sawing out a section of the reel's back plate to expose the inner flange of the spool, thereby allowing ample space for finger control. Today, a rim-control Pfleuger fly reel is available, but most anglers still prefer to use the modified version of the original pattern.

Since those initial make-do times, many top reel-manufacturers have designed and developed reels that have become standard production. The British firm Hardy produces a fine reel, as does Fin-Nor in the USA. Billy Pate, the doyen of tarpon anglers, markets a magnificent saltwater fly reel, and one enterprising family business also produces one-piece, customized aluminium spools for the old-style Pfleuger Medalist reels.

Once anglers realized that they could subdue the mighty tarpon on fly tackle, they turned their attentions to other species. Until this time they had confined their fly-fishing activities to inshore waters. Now the thinking turned seawards. Obvious predators like dolphin fish and small tuna were the first species tried for, and both proved to be perfect fly-rod targets, providing the speedy action that the fly-rodders craved for. For a time the anglers had been satisfied that they had conquered the hard-hitting inshore species. Then the high-jumping dolphin fish and the depth-seeking tuna had brought them offshore. Now the sky was the limit. What they all dreamed of was taking billfish and high-jumping mako shark on the fly rod. The dream that no angler had believed could become reality suddenly became an established fact.

First came the sailfish on fly; then it was the turn of the white, the blue and the striped marlin; finally, the mako shark fell to custom-tied lures and popping bugs. It was soon realized that it was not practical to cruise across the ocean in the hope of finding a billfish to cast at. Instead, anglers started to tow hookless lures to entice the billfish to the surface. Once a fish came up, the lures were pulled in and a big fly was dropped back to the fish. Often such tactics produced a smash take, as the angry fish, robbed of its first food choice, smashed into the only thing left that looked edible. By this stage the saltwater flies were big, bulky and garish creations, but they caught fish. The late Lee Wulff, always one for refinement, took the whole thing a stage further and took a sailfish on a so-called dry fly.

Saltwater fly-casting is natural for American anglers, who have a wealth of fish from which to choose but what of we Europeans? We have no big game species except porbeagle shark and no exotic inshore fish. What we do have, however, is a range of fish that will take lure-type flies. Mackerel, garfish, pollack, coalfish and bass all can and will hit a fast-moving flashy lure, and, because none of these are really big fish, they can all be handled on a standard reservoir fly rod and line with additional backing. They all swim close to the rocky coastline or around piers and harbours, and this means that they are potential sport for the fly-rodder. The rugged coast of Ireland, west Scotland and Cornwall are ideal places to try fly fishing, and the rock marks of Brittany and the Channel Islands are also well suited to the sport. On a light outfit casting a 5/6 sinking line, even the humble mackerel or aerobatic garfish turn into miniature big game species, and pollack and coalfish, although not as fiery, certainly pull their weight. When heavy pollack or bass are known

to be in the area it is advisable to step up the weight of the tackle. A 9ft or 10ft rod throwing a number 9 line is near perfect. All in all, saltwater casting is established in the USA and could, in time, become a standard practice in Britain and Europe. As a technique it has much to offer and presents a new and fascinating angle to the sea-angler.

19
BONEFISH

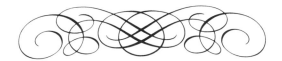

BY BIG FISH standards the bonefish (*Albula vulpes*) is a tiddler. A big one may weigh 15lb and the average for the species is 3–6 lb. What the bonefish lacks in size, however, it more than makes up for in elusiveness, speed and tenacity. Once described as the 'fastest thing on fins', bonefish have long since established themselves as a 'must' for the light-tackle enthusiast. Fly-rodding for bonefish has become a standard technique, and the angler who has successfully hooked and subdued a big bonefish on fly tackle can enter the ranks of the sport fishing élite.

From a fishing point of view, the Florida keys, the Bahama flats and the wild coast of Yucatán and Belize are the world's bonefish hot-spots, and many anglers automatically assume that bonefish are a wholly shallow-water species. This is far from the truth, and off Hawaii and other islands really huge bonefish are found in deep water where they can be taken on conventional bottom-fishing tackle and baits. These huge fish seldom venture out of the depths to feed on the inshore shallows, however, so the shallow, sun-warmed coral flats are the places to head for in the hope of some bonefish action. The Florida Keys are a typical location. The Keys form a 200-mile long archipelago, curving southwest from the bustle of Miami, starting at the entrance to Biscayne Bay and ending at Key West. Seawards, they face on to the deep water blue of the Florida Straits; on the opposite, Florida Bay side, the huge shallow flats, representing around 4,000 square miles of shoal water, provide some of the greatest shallow-water fishing in the world. The Bahamas, with an estimated 70,000 square miles of coral flats, are another fine bonefish area. These Bahama island flats are said to be the most extensive bonefish grounds in the world. Compared with the Bahamas, the bonefish grounds of Yucatán and Belize are small, and what they lack in size, they make up for in quantity of fish, bird life and fascinating mangrove jungle with its fish-filled saltwater creeks. Where else in the world could you fish for the speedy bonefish under the awe-inspiring architecture of a long-deserted Mayan temple? No matter where you fish, these vast areas of sparkling shoal waters rank high among the world's most beautiful fishing grounds. The passing of a single cloud across the flats can change the colours of the sea through a startling range of pastel greens and blues that no artist could even hope to capture with paint and canvas.

Of the many fish camps that specialize in bonefish, one of the most pleasant is Deepwater Cay, Grand Bahama, where a tiny collection of rondavel-type cottages surrounds the club house. Deepwater Cay is built on a spit of sand and coral rock, surrounded on all sides by mile after magic mile of bonefish flats. Each morning anglers load their tackle and food into a sleek, bow-platformed bonefish skiff to surge through miles of mangrove creeks in search of the ever-secretive bonefish. Heavy-duty outboard engines are used to cut down travelling time until the guide reaches the chosen fishing area. Then the engines are cut, tilted and secured. From then on the boat is propelled by pole and muscle, so that the ever-wary bonefish are not alarmed. The guides know their areas inside out, and they pole silently through long, shiny-leafed corridors of clutching mangroves to reach long-hidden flats where bonefish may be found.

Small bonefish have a tendency to shoal, each shoal containing a hundred or more fish. Hook one fish, and the rest of the shoal will follow its every twist, turn or long dash for freedom. The effect is startling – it is almost as if the entire shoal was on the one hook, a vast mass of running fish attached to a single line. Only when the hooked fish begins to tire does the shoal lose interest, disappearing across the flats in search of fresh feeding grounds. The larger fish tend to become solitary, and a rich feeding area may attract a number of big bonefish, each acting and feeding as an individual. This is where fish have to be sighted, stalked and cast to accurately. Initially, the novice to bonefish angling will have trouble spotting the fish. It seems hard to look at clear, shallow water and not be able to see a creature that the guide has long since spotted. After a few days, eyes become capable of picking out the ghostly grey shadows, or even the flicker of fins. At first, however, this is impossible, and, knowing this, the guide will give clear and precise instructions as to the position and distance of the feeding fish. 'Sixty feet at 11 o'clock,' is a typical example. At this stage the angler must not hesitate, wasting

valuable seconds straining to see the fish. The cast should be made instantly to coincide exactly with the guide's instructions.

The splash of the falling bait or the glint of the fly is enough to attract the attention of the browsing fish, and, if all goes well, the fish will be hooked up in seconds. Then look out! Thoroughly alarmed, the bonefish will take off as though supercharged. It is no use worrying then whether the knots are right or if there is enough line or backing on the reel. The hooked fish may take 150 yards of line in seconds. If the angler can live through this first high-speed rush, the hooked bonefish should start to turn in a wide semi-circle before starting off again at a new angle. The guide will help by poling rapidly after the retreating fish. This enables the angler to gain line rapidly. At no time must the bonefish be allowed slack line. These fish have a leathery mouth, and, if the hook is not deeply embedded, it may drop out as the line slackens. If all goes well, each run should grow shorter, until the guide can lean over and net the obviously tired fish. The weights of most bonefish are quickly estimated, so that they can be quickly unhooked, photographed and returned alive.

Many anglers new to bonefish make the mistake of deciding on a single technique long before they arrive at the chosen bonefish camp. They often decide to fish fly only and pack nothing but fly-fishing tackle. It is, however, better to catch a fish or three on jig baits or natural baits to get a feel of the bonefish and to get the eyes adjusted to the deceptive glimmer of the fish as they sift through the coral marl. Jigging with tiny lead-head jigs is an effective way of catching fish, but for observing the bonefish and its reactions natural baits are advisable. In the wild, bonefish feed on tiny fish, crabs, shrimps and the tough flesh of the conch. Frozen shrimp is the easiest and most natural of hook baits to use, and it should be used on a light spinning rod and fixed-spool reel, loaded with 8 or 10lb b.s. line. No additional weights are used on the line, the weight of the bait being sufficient for casting purposes. During the first day or two the anglers have to rely on the guide's eyesight and instructions. Then, when they can spot fish for themselves, the juicy shrimp can be cast to drop ahead of the feeding fish so that it can be watched and studied as it approaches and takes the shrimp. Once the eyes have adjusted, the clarity of the water will show every detail of both fish and bait.

When the angler can see the fish clearly, the fly rod can be assembled with confidence. American bonefish flies tend to be roughly tied on heavy hooks, each fly being designed to resemble a shrimp

or small crab. The keen fly dresser can, however, easily make up a selection of far better patterns, although it must be remembered that the jaws of a bonefish are designed to crush natural prey. For this reason, heavier hooks should be used. For most fly-fishing conditions a 9ft 6in or 10ft fly rod, designed to cast a number 8 or number 9 line is perfectly adequate. The reel, however, should be chosen carefully. First, it must be large enough to take a weight-forward floating line plus a minimum of 150 yards of 20lb Dacron backing. In addition, and as important, the reel must be capable of withstanding the ravages of saltwater. Corrosion destroys reels in days rather than in weeks. Many good patterns are available, particularly in the USA. Leaders should be rod length, and they should be cut from a spool of 10 or 12lb nylon.

When the fly-fishing stage is reached, the fish can be stalked in conventional manner, either by spotting fish feeding over the marl or by watching for the elegant, white tail flag of an up-ended bonefish. Once sighted, the cast should be made so that the fly lands just ahead of the feeding fish. The bonefish often spots the fly as it drops through the clear water, and, when this happens, it may move forwards to intercept the fly as it falls. Failing this, the fly should be allowed to settle, then twitched back, so that at each tiny pull it sends up a tiny spurt of coral marl. Bonefish expect crab and shrimp to give themselves away in this fashion, and so will normally surge forward to suck in the fly. Once hooked, the bonefish will take off on a swift run that will empty the reel spool of line and most of the backing in seconds. More than one fly-rodder has run out of backing line and has been forced to jump overboard to run after the fleeing fish. Bonefish may not be in the heavyweight class, but they are capable of fly-weight action than can make many other fish look like sloths. Wherever bonefish exist there will be fishermen who would rather catch a single bonefish than a host of salmon or even a mighty marlin.

20
WAHOO

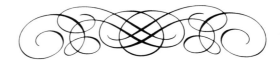

THE WAHOO (*Acanthocybium solandri*) may average only 20–40lb in weight, but what it lacks in size it more than makes up for in speed and endurance. Essentially a light-tackle species, the wahoo occurs in tropical seas around the world. The largest rod-caught wahoo weighed in at 149lb, but a fish of this size is an exception to all the rules. To catch a wahoo weighing more than 80lb is unusual. The name wahoo is said to have come from the cowboy yell of the first angler to set a hook into the species. How much truth there is in this story no one really knows – like most angling yarns, there must be some truth in the origin of the name, but over the years, no doubt, the original story has been improved and embellished by succeeding generations. One thing is certain: the hard-hitting, hard-fighting wahoo is an established favourite with all saltwater game fishermen.

Wahoo are highly predatory raiders, which hunt reefs and the open sea. Their technique is to run their quarry down and cut it in half with their strange crescent-shaped teeth. Anglers who have fished in wahoo country will confirm that the fish seems to have an uncanny ability to chop a natural bait off directly behind the hook. To do this so accurately, the fish must have both the speed and the eyesight to see the bait and the hidden hook in minute detail. Wahoo will also strike fast-moving artificial lures. Kona Heads, Hawaiian Eyes and Japanese Feathers all attract and catch wahoo. Unfortunately, the fish's sharp teeth often destroy the skirts of expensive lures, but wahoo that strike at artificials hook themselves in the process.

Although they are always ready to strike at surface level, the wahoo is, in fact, a sub-surface raider. For this reason the heavy, lead-headed Japanese Feathers often catch better than more ornate surface lures. A trolled Japanese Feather will normally out-fish other lures at a ratio of four strikes to one. In most areas, wahoo are taken by accident on lures intended for billfish or tuna. This is a pity, for it means that most of these magnificent fish are taken on heavy tackle, which gives them little opportunity to show their true fighting spirit. There are places, however, where wahoo are so common that they can be fished for on a deliberate basis. These wahoo strongholds are nearly always located off volcanic islands – Madeira, for example, has large stocks of heavyweight wahoo, fish averaging 70–90lb.

Another wahoo island is lonely Ascension Island, in the South Atlantic. Ascension Island is at present in the hands of NATO forces, and its teeming waters seldom get fished on a serious basis. Ascension Island looks like a typical volcanic island when it is seen from the sea. Old volcanic craters and lava-flow cliffs make it look

stonily attractive. Inland, however, it is a different story. Two hundred years of military occupation has left its scars on an already bleak landscape. The bird life is almost non-existent, and the sparse vegetation supports only a few emaciated donkeys and long-neglected sheep. The only green and cultivated spot is high on a volcanic peak known as Green Mountain. Traditionally the home of the island's governors, Green Mountain was created and landscaped during the last century. Originally as bleak, barren and windswept as the rest of the island, this verdant peak was overlaid with millions of tons of rich African topsoil, which was transported from mainland Africa by sailing ship then carried laboriously in baskets by the local garrison. The journey across the lava flows must have taken days. To provide rough shelter for the marines, old lifeboats were stood on end at strategic points – the forerunners of today's one-boat and two-boat dormitory towns, used exclusively by the armed forces. Having no natural population of its own, the island relies on labour from St Helena, 800 miles to the south. The 'Saints', as they are called, reside around the rudimentary harbour, Georgetown. Almost every cove on the island has its tiny cluster of graves, the resting places of countless victims of yellow fever, who were unloaded by the captains of passing sailing ships, bound to and from the fever-ridden ports of Africa, India and beyond, and left to die in isolated misery.

Ascension, then, is not an attractive island, but its fishing must rate as, potentially, among the best in the world. There are plenty of yellow-fin tuna to be had, and the billfish population is enormous. The few boats that have managed to get offshore have contacted massive sailfish and lost more than their fair share of blue marlin. This is trolling country, and, in the absence of natural baits, artificial lures are essential. The wahoo are taken within half to one mile from the barren cliffs, and, even this close, the water is deep, incredibly clear and unaccountably cold. Ascension Island may be situated off the steamy west coast of Africa, but little of Africa finds its way into the south Atlantic.

When I fished in Ascension Island waters, the weather was a heady mixture of storm, sun and constant wind. On land, the air was warm and the frequent heavy rain a cooling relief. Offshore, the seas were rough and the wind had a bite to it. Despite this, fish were everywhere – yellow-fin tuna to 180lb, huge, hard-hitting jacks and the fast-moving wahoo. As always the wahoo preferred to feed at sub-surface levels. They would come up to chop at a Kona Head, which usually resulted in a spoiled plastic skirt. Fortunately, I had brought a plentiful supply of lead-headed Japanese Feathers.

Game fish have their colour likes and dislikes. Barracuda prefer yellow. Tuna like black. Wahoo like red and white, and, no matter where you go in the world, wahoo will take these colours. Ascension Island wahoo were typical of their breed. Crimp on a red and white lure, and the boat would not have travelled half a mile before the rod tip was wrenched down and the Shimano multiplier began to scream. Initially, a hooked wahoo is confident that its speed is enough to break free of the restraining tackle. Once it realizes that these tactics are not enough, it will turn down in a zigzag fighting style, for which muscle rather than overall speed is used. This fighting technique can be violently effective. The continual shift in speed and angle can easily jar the carefully sharpened hook free. As always, the lure was fished on a short wire trace, incorporating a matt black swivel. Far too many anglers use a shiny silver swivel, and they lose the trace and lure, or, worse, the trace, lure and fish, to a wahoo that hits the swivel thinking it is a tiny bait fish. Black swivels do not seem to trigger the killer instinct in predatory fish. Silver is a clear signal to strike and kill, but black seems to be ignored. Like wahoo the world over, the Ascension Island fish use their speed to intercept and 'kill' any lure that attracts their attention. Once hooked, they can be guaranteed to fight like demons.

One day the soldiers will leave Ascension Island, and it is certain to become a great centre for sport fishermen. When this day comes, wahoo records could be quickly rewritten. In the last few years global warming has allowed the wahoo – and many other species – to extend their habitat range and colonize new areas. The Azores are a typical example of an island group where wahoo were once unknown but are now a resident species. At present the Bahamas, the Cayman Islands, Cozumel and Yucatán are all wahoo hot-spots, and the coast of Kenya also produces many fine specimens. The wahoo, then, is a very available species that is likely to become more so. Although few anglers actually set out to catch wahoo, it can only be a matter of time before anglers gear down and set their sights on this species. Not only is the wahoo a beautifully coloured and shaped species, it is also a great table fish. Butterfly steaks of firm wahoo meat are prized wherever the fish occurs.

21
PERMIT

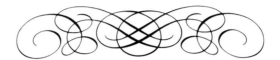

FOR OVER TWO hours the skiff had been flying through endless corridors of overhanging mangroves. Initially stimulating, mangrove jungle soon becomes a seemingly never-changing curtain of drab green. Even the saltwater rivers, which twist and turn through this wilderness, have little to recommend them. Occasionally the dull splat of a jumping fish or a shower of panicked bait fish breaks up the boredom, but usually little else occurs to alleviate the overall stifling blanket effect. Suddenly, however, it all changes. One moment there is a never-ending vista of uniform, dark green foliage, the next, we streak out into golden sunlight. Ahead lies a vast saltwater lake, with just the occasional small island to break up the waiting expanse. Still the engine roars and the expressionless Mayan Indian guide keeps his hand firmly on the tiller. He knows where he is going and he does not feel that he needs to explain it to the two anglers amidships. We know we are on a permit fishing expedition, so we simply rely on the inscrutable Mayan to put us on fish.

Strapped along the gunwhales are four made-up rods. There is a pair of short American spin casters, matched with Shimano fixed-spool reels. Only the best reels are good enough for the speedy permit (*Trachinotus falcatus*). Each reel is fully loaded with new 10lb b.s. nylon, and to the end of each line is tied an ugly little lead-headed jig. These jigs look like tiny, flat frogs with painted eyes and a bushy tail, but in the water they will look like tiny sand crabs. Permit love to gorge on crabs, and these lures are just what the fish want – at least, that is what they told us back at Boca Paila lodge. The other rods are a matching pair of 9ft carbon fly rods, each equipped with a large fly reel carrying a full number 9 weight-forward fly line, 150 yards of 20lb backing line and a 10lb test leader. The fly, a simple

imitation of a shrimp, might not look much out of the water but twitched over the sea bed it has brought about the downfall of many a hefty permit.

The permit on the flats of Yucatán tend to live and feed around the lovely blue holes. A blue hole is basically the mouth of an underwater tunnel linking the interior salt flats with the open ocean many miles away. Such holes are clearly visible, as their depth turns the water a lovely violet-blue. There is an up-thrust of water in the hole that creates a gentle but obvious boiling effect on the surface, and presumably this up-thrust must bring some food with it, for the

permit patrol the edges of the caverns, and they can often be seen cruising about in search of food. Occasionally they make brief forays out over the shallow flats that surround the perimeter of the blue hole.

Long before we got to the first fishing hole, our guide cut the motor and used a long pole to propel the boat silently forwards. Permit are easily spooked, quick to vanish at the first sign of disturbance. When we were at a distance of about 80ft from the hole, the guide stopped the boat and indicated that we should pick up the jig-casting rods because there were two permit on the lip of the blue hole, possibly on their way out over the coral marl. I could not see the fish at first, then suddenly there they were – two dark, wandering shapes, browsing slowly along a line of yellow-orange weed. Gradually the fish parted company, one setting a slow but steady course out and away from the blue hole, the other fish, more cautious, wandering away from the weed line but keeping within easy range of the indigo blue of the tunnel mouth. This gave us both a chance to try for a permit.

The technique of jig-fishing for permit is to cast ahead and beyond the fish, then to retrieve in short, sharp jerks. This causes the lead-bodied jig to hop across the sea bed, each jump raising a tiny cloud of coral marl. The spurts of silt make the jig look like a tiny crab or sand shrimp, both of which figure on the permit's daily diet sheet. With this in mind, I cast to drop my jig beyond and about two yards in front of my target fish. Two quick jerks and the fish was on the jig. I was not close enough to see it suck in the lure, but I saw it dart forwards, and I struck automatically. Permit on the cruise may look dumpy and incapable of serious action, but set a hook into one and things change dramatically. A hooked permit shifts into high gear in a split second. One moment it is idling along, the next it is streaking across the flats, taking line at a speed that has to be seen to be believed. My fish bolted as expected, at first running far out across the shallows and taking at least 150 yards of line off the spool. Abruptly it turned at right angles, then swung back, heading straight for the sanctuary of the blue hole.

Fortunately, the initial disturbance had badly frightened the second permit, so there was no fear of two lines crossing. With this worry off my mind, I was able to concentrate all my attention on the running fish. I knew that if it reached the lip of the blue hole it would crash dive into the tunnel proper and the line would part on the coral rock. At one stage it was within a few feet of its objective, but I was able to turn it. It instantly set off across the flats, but it was obviously tiring, and minutes later it was in the net. Yucatán permit are not monsters, and this one weighed an estimated 12lb. After the hook was removed it was photographed and returned, and at the last sighting it vanished into dark indigo-blue water for a well-earned rest.

There were several blue holes in the vicinity, and our Mayan guide poled us gently across to the nearest. Sure enough, as the skiff came to a halt, we could see a single large permit on station just inside the crater's lip. Interestingly, quite a flow of water was coming out of the hole – from the boat it looked as if the water was boiling. This was a fly-casting situation. My fishing companion was, to say the least, an accomplished fly-caster and was soon double-hauling to gain distance. The fly was a bulky American shrimp imitation, which, by European standards, was poorly tied. Despite this, it was highly thought of locally and had apparently accounted for plenty of good permit. With the fish virtually stationary, it was easy to drop the fly ahead and beyond it. Once it had sunk beneath the surface, a couple of long pulls brought it within range of the waiting permit. The second it came into its line of sight, the lounging permit seemed to bristle with anticipation – it seemed to sit up and pay attention. It simply shaped up, every fin quivering. One more pull was enough. The permit shot forward and nailed the fly, obviously hooking itself in the process. Instantly it went into a rolling dive, which took it down out of sight. For a second or two, it looked as though it would go to ground in the blue depths. Then it changed tactics, shot across the hole and took off as though its tail was on fire. No reel can scream like a fly reel under stress. Within seconds the fly line and half the backing sped through the rod rings. Fortunately, the guide was used to permit tactics, and he deftly poled the skiff around the hole and out on to the golden shadows of the flats. Here, the fish fought magnificently against the power of the rod and drag of line and backing. Long minutes later it was circling towards the big landing net. By Yucatán standards this was a real specimen, weighing 18–20lb. Soon it was back in the water, tired but game enough to swim slowly off in the direction of the blue hole.

Two permit in a day is a good result. It is not that the fish is rare – Florida guides have reported permit by the thousand – but by angling standards a boated permit must rate as one of the rarest game fish in the world. Wily and disinclined to feed, the scary permit is, at best, a difficult fish to tempt, and once hooked a permit will try every trick in the book in a serious attempt to snag the line or dislodge the offending hook.

Young permit are often confused with pompano. The adult permit are bluish-grey on the back, the body is silvery, and the dorsal and tail have black anterior margins. Mostly seen in small schools, permit often trail along behind feeding sting ray. The wallowing ray excavate pits in their search for food, and this action often turns up molluscs and crabs, providing the crafty permit pack with easy pickings. The vast flats of Yucatán are thick with the huge, slimy sting ray. Although it is hardly a pack fish, the ray will gather in numbers in a potentially food rich area, and, normally the permit will be in close attendance.

If you want to see really large permit, the Florida Keys is the place to head for. In the Bahamas, Deepwater Cay can provide the chance to catch good fish. Permit fishing is not for the faint-hearted, however. It is mostly a frustrating mixture of lost opportunities and lost fish. On the right day, when just for once everything goes right and the angler hits the jackpot, all those lost days fade from the memory. Permit fever takes over, and the whole business starts again. Few anglers have caught more than thirty permit in a lifetime's fishing, and it is almost a masochistic sport, in which the angler inflicts maximum physical and mental punishment on himself. Catch just one, however, and you are lost. Permit addicts abound. Consistently successful permit fishermen are as rare as hen's teeth.

22
TARPON

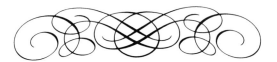

ONE OF THE greatest challenges to the light-tackle angler, the tarpon (*Megalops atlantica*) is the big game fish of the inshore shallows. Little more than a century ago, tarpon were regarded as uncatchable, unstoppable monsters that were best left alone. Then a totally unknown angler, W.H. Wood from New York, took a Florida tarpon weighing 93lb. This fish is a baby by today's standards, but it started a Klondyke-like rush to fish the mangrove wilderness that we now call the Florida Keys. The fishing was not easy: the tackle was primitive, the reels had to be braked by leather pads or thumbstalls, and the rods of the day were stiff and unyielding. Above all, the fish were wild and strong. Three- and four-hour battles were commonplace and usually ended in lost fish and the angler needing medical attention. 'Hook ups' were easy, few fish were boated and discouragement was in the air. Then, in 1898, Edward Vonn Hofe, a New York reel-maker, put a magnificent 210-pounder in the boat. This unbelievable fish was taken at Captiva Pacs.

Since that historic day, tarpon weighing up to nearly 300lb have been taken, and larger fish are known to exist. Obviously, as the quality of tackle improved, anglers began to take tarpon on a regular basis, and today's angler can now take a tarpon-fishing holiday and expect to make constant contact with large specimens. Tarpon occur in all tropical, sub-tropical and temperate areas of the Atlantic, but they are probably commonest in Florida, although off the Mexican coast the fish can be found as far down as Panama. Strangely, they have never become established in Pacific waters.

Tarpon are at their best in river mouths, where the water is less saline than the open ocean. Like most wild creatures, they suffer quickly from pollution and man-made disturbances. The coast of Texas is a typical example. This was once a noted venue for large tarpon, but marine disturbances caused the stocks to vanish, and, although tarpon shoals still visit the area, they are not seen in the numbers this coast once produced. The destruction of the inshore nursery areas creates havoc with localized tarpon populations, because tarpon spawn offshore and the larvae slowly drift inshore, remaining in the shallow water until they attain a length of 25–30in. Pollution, construction and general disturbance have destroyed many of the main tarpon nursery areas. One of the few existing safe havens for the developing tarpon is the Everglades National Park.

Once the young fish return to the open sea they have a lifespan of from ten to fifteen years. The real giants tend to stay in the sea, but fish weighing 15–20lb often penetrate inland by means of river and canal systems. In the Cayman Islands these fish seem to thrive in the mosquito canals and even in tiny land-locked ponds. Such fish can never hope to return to the sea, which shows that tarpon can tolerate and adapt to life in both brackish and almost fresh, even stagnant, water. These land-locked Cayman Islands tarpon seldom grow to any great size, but they attract a lot of attention from visiting anglers. The mosquito canals are badly overgrown, and the only real way to catch fish is to plug-fish with brightly coloured, jointed Rapala type lures.

Fishing for large tarpon has become a science. These giant herrings can be taken on surface plug baits, live mullet and a variety of other live fish baits. Real tarpon anglers, however, prefer to fly-fish. Even before the turn of the century, small tarpon were being taken on fly rods, and rods of greenheart, lancewood and even split cane were in constant use, although not against the real giants of the tribe. These early rods and reels were not powerful enough to subdue a really big fish – and worse, anglers were fighting from rowing boats or even canoes, cockleshells that could be towed for miles with the fish firmly in control and the angler and boatman hanging on for grim death. Accidents were common, boats were overturned, and fish even jumped into boats. Early tarpon fishing was a rough, tough sport, which produced a great many disappointments and only the occasional success.

Today the scene has changed, and it now favours the angler. Modern, high-powered skiffs can be used to outrun fighting fish, space-age rod materials can take massive amounts of punishment while applying maximum pressure to the hooked tarpon, and custom reel designs, with complex drag systems, take a lot of the work out of playing a big tarpon.

The type and weight of the fly tackle in general use is dictated by the size of fish that can be expected. For most of the canal systems a 9ft rod, capable of throwing a size 8 weight-forward line is perfectly adequate. Down in the Florida Keys or on the coast, where much larger fish may be encounted, a 9ft 6in graphite, boron or Kevlar rod, capable of casting a size 12 weight-forward floating line, is more in keeping with the size of in-running tarpon. These rods are matched with customized reels from Billy Pate or Fin-Nor or the Hardy Ocean Prince – heavy-duty fly reels, fitted with multi-disc or large disc-type drags and capable of maintaining a constant setting. The reel must be large enough to hold 250 to 300 yards of Dacron-type backing, plus a full-length fly line. Most keen tarpon anglers like to use leaders in 8, 12 or 16lb b.s. for everyday angling, while first-time tarpon anglers are advised to have a 16lb b.s. leader. Tarpon have hard, abrasive mouths which rapidly chaff through light line, and for this reason a 12in length of 60 or 80lb b.s. nylon should be firmly knotted to the end of the actual leader. Long leaders are not necessary, and most experienced tarpon men use a length of nylon that corresponds to the length of the rod. Some anglers prefer to use a tapered leader, made of 5ft of 40lb nylon, or 16lb nylon and 12in of 60 80lb nylon.

Flies are tied on the streamer pattern, and only a few are designed to imitate live food. Taking colours change from day to day, and anglers carry a wide range of patterns or colours. Some flies have typically outlandish names – Blue Roach, Pink Fluff, Midnite Blue, Chinese Claw, Blue Death, and so on – and the amateur fly-tier can let his creative skills take over in the never-ending search for the ultimate pattern.

Tarpon fishing depends greatly on the incoming tide. A typical day starts at around 8 o'clock in the morning, with the skiff anchored in only a few feet of water. The guide will choose a typical tarpon alley, a place tarpon are known to visit on a regular basis, although, like all fishing, nothing is guaranteed and luck plays an important part in any day's fishing. The tarpon fisher has to play a waiting game, staked out in the hot sun, waiting and hoping that the fish will come as the tide continues to rise. For hours the surface may be broken only by the ever-present mullet shoals. Suddenly, a batch of sweeping shadows will cruise into view. Shadows that push a huge bow wave ahead of them. Occasionally a great scaly back will break water, or a mighty fish will surge sideways to intercept a luckless mullet. This is when the knees begin to shake. Often the guide will have seen the fish long before the angler realizes that the moment of truth is nearly on hand. Instructions are always given against the imaginary hour markings of a clock face. 'Big fish at 11.30, casting distance 70 feet,' whispers the guide. The angler has no time to waste. If he cannot see the fish himself, he must take the guide's word for it. With the minimum of false casting, the fly is on its way, and now everything is in the lap of the sea-gods.

The second the streamer fly sinks, the angler must start stripping back line. The tarpon is on the hunt and any swift movement will catch its eye and, the angler hopes, register as food in its brain. If the streamer is seen and the fish is interested, it will change gears in a fraction of a second and close its vast mouth solidly over the frantically moving fly. Then watch out. Big tarpon may look lethargic as they idle on the surface, but, once they feel the hook and line drag, they go berserk, leaping skyward, with gills rattling and broad tail beating the surface water to foam. If these tactics fail, the fish will start to run, causing the reel to scream and the backing line to vanish as if by magic. Throughout this activity, the angler must hang on, thinking through each stage of the prolonged battle. If the fish runs to the right, the rod must be pulled round to the left. If it turns left, the rod must instantly come round to the right to apply maximum pressure. If, which is rarely the case, the fish runs straight ahead, the rod must be kept high and well bent. The second the tarpon explodes from the water the rod tip must be dropped to water level. This creates slack line and may save the day if the fish falls back on the leader. Only by keeping the pressure on can the angler hope to fight the tarpon to a standstill. This means applying constant and maximum rod pressure to the breaking point of the thinnest leader section.

Under no circumstances should the fish be brought to the boat unless it is totally exhausted. More than one allegedly played-out tarpon has suddenly come alive, wrecking the boat in the process. Even worse occurs when the guide gaffs a 'green' fish and gets dragged overboard in the process. The gaff is used only when a fish is going to be brought ashore. Most anglers and their guides are happy to snip the leader and let the fish go, guessing its weight before it is released. The beauty of the catch-and-release system is that the angler has all the fun of the fighting and the memory of the fish at the moment of release. More important still, that fish has been given its freedom, to live, spawn and maybe fight again on another day.

23
THE MAKING OF
A YOUNG ANGLER

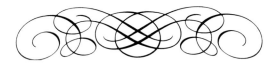

HAVING A SON who wants to fish puts immense responsibility on a father's shoulders. The natural reaction is to bring the boy into fishing at adult level: why mess around with tiddlers when you can catch a big fish is the theory. But like most theories, this one is seriously flawed. For a start, adult fishing is an unutterably slow and boring pastime for a child. What the average child wants is to go out on a nice day and haul an endless succession of struggling tiddlers out of the water. Size and species are immaterial – it is quantity that counts. Quality can come later.

As a professional angler who became a father rather late in the day, the last seven years have been something of a revelation. From the age of four onwards my son showed an interest in fishing that was almost an obsession. As long as he was by water, he was happy only when he was trying to catch something. Fortunately, I had seen the mistakes angling friends had made. Too many budding fishermen had been dragged off on the search for that 'glass-case' monster, which would set them up in the eyes of their father and his admiring friends. The results of such thinking have always been disastrous. Usually the child sees and catches nothing, and rapidly becomes bored with the whole idea. If he has caught a good fish, the glory is short lived; anything of lesser size is an anticlimax. Whatever happens, the world loses a future angler.

My belief is that a child should serve the sort of angling apprenticeship that all real anglers have gone through. With this in mind, I rolled back the years and started at the beginning. Half the fun of catching fish comes from tinkering with the tackle, so we began by laboriously converting a plastic lemonade bottle into a rough but serviceable minnow trap. With a plastic bucket and a chunk of bread we headed for the nearest stream. The trap was a success – the bucket was filled with bright little minnows, both of us got water down our boots, and neither of us cared. We had set out on a quest and had succeeded beyond all expectations. The bucket of minnows was living proof that, as a partnership, we made a good team. Those minnows lived out their life in an aquarium that served as a mirror for a lifetime of fishing expectations.

From the minnow trap it was but a short step to more grandiose plans. A lightweight telescopic rod arrived from Father Christmas, and endless plans were made for the fishing to come, plans that meant that I had to change my lifestyle. Normally, I would be out of the country for most of the year, but now I had to cut down my big game expeditions by half. I had made promises, and the easiest way to break a child's heart and hope is by reneging on a promise. A father's word is his bond and he had better stick to it. Not for me the endless blue seas and palm-cloaked beaches. My dreams of marlin and tuna were swapped for an endless stream of four-to-the-pound coarse fish. I still managed to squeeze in a few trips, but even then I felt guilty and longed for the muddy ponds and the endless stream of chatter from a happy boy who just wanted to fish.

Time passed, and in the next few years we moved on from tiddler bashing to trotting bright red worm for the obliging grayling. This led gradually to an awareness of trout and the insects that they feed on. Father Christmas seemed to know that a fly-tying kit was needed. What excitement and what horrors were created by those unskilled fingers. I admired and boxed five-minute creations that would never catch fish. Constant encouragement brought the ultimate rewards of patience and increased skill. Now the fly patterns were good enough to catch trout, and it was my job to cast and hook fish. The rod was then passed over, and I stood by with the net. This arrangement continued for several seasons, until the boy was tall enough and competent enough to cast to his own fish, although success was still measured in bag limits rather than size of fish caught.

Soon, I was taking the boy on shark fishing expeditions. While I fished for shark, he did the more important job of catching mackerel as baits. As it was put to me: 'the best angler in the world won't catch fish without fresh bait.' And I could not refute the logic of that. Then, when he was ten, I went out to Kenya to fish in a tournament. Enthusiastic about the trip, I told him of the golden African beaches, the blue of the Indian Ocean, the passing dhows and the bright colours of the rich and varied reef fish. Too late, I realized that I had done the wrong thing. He still asked questions, but not with the same eagerness as before. We had fished together so much that he couldn't bear to hear of my experiences and successes. I made a silent promise: no matter what happened, I would take him back the following sailfish season. He had every right to experience the screaming reel, bucking rod and the pull of a high-jumping sailfish. He should see the glowing colours of the great sail and feel the roughness of the long beak. It was his right to catch a big game fish, and I felt he was ready to make a giant leap in his angling career. After much planning and secrecy it was arranged. I broke the news on his eleventh birthday. From then on it was fact: Dad said he was going to Africa, and Dad kept his promise. At this time I was living on borrowed time. I was already well past my sell-by date and was feeling it. The boy knew the situation, but he also knew we would go.

Finally, we were on the way. A night flight from a misty, damp England to a dawn awakening, with the sun rising over the rift valley and Mount Kilimanjaro. Soon we were through the uproar of Mombasa airport and heading up the coast to Hemingway's Hotel at Watamu near Malindi. As soon as we arrived, we hurried down to explore the hotel, the beach and the exposed rock pools. The plaster casts of fish on the hotel walls had to be studied carefully and at great length. Then came the flood of questions. Was the dorsal fin of the sailfish as blue as the one on the wall? How does the fish strike the bait? And so on. I had a boat booked the next day, and at 5.30 in the morning we were down for a quick breakfast then out to the boat for a 6.30 start. Within the hour the boy had caught a dolphin fish, a *falusi* as it is known in Kenya. At 10lb it was the biggest thing he had ever caught. The adventure had started, and it was all true.

By 10 o'clock he had caught a batch of hard-hitting bonito and we were working well offshore. Our target was a sailfish. For a while nothing, then out of nowhere came a strike. This was no billfish – it didn't jump, it simply dived. With the boy in the chair, hanging on for grim death, I could only hang on to his shoulder harness and give advice. Initially, we had thought the fish was a 22lb yellow-fin tuna, but we quickly realized that it was a much larger specimen. Big tuna are brutal fish to fight, but the boy stood all the lunges that ripped hundreds of feet of line from the protesting reel. He must have been hurting, but didn't show it. Instead, he took all the punishment the

fish handed out and gave it some stick for its trouble. Every fight must end, but this one took nearly an hour before the gaff struck home. Later that yellow-fin weighed in at 111½lb – many pounds heavier than the newly arrived big game angler who had caught it. What made it better was that it was larger than any yellow-fin tuna that I had caught.

The next day we were up again before dawn, heading out in the hope of some sailfish action. Soon the boy had a nice barracuda in the boat and we trolled on over an indigo-blue sea. Then a good sailfish surged up behind a bait and the fight was on. After the tuna experience the boy knew what to expect and set to in earnest. Even now, after many years of catching huge billfish, I am still surprised by the riot of vivid, high-leaping colour. To the boy this must have seemed a magical fish – the vivid blue dorsal fin, electric blue bars and tail and all the wildness that makes a game fish so special. I was praying that the hook would hold. I had seen too many billfish jump off, and to lose his first sailfish would be a tragedy for the boy. Fortunately, he fought it like a veteran. Plenty of rod pressure and short pumps before a rapid wind down. Every yard of line gained was a success, and it was soon apparent that he would boat this fish. I knew his dearest ambition was to have the bill of his first sail as a trophy, and who could blame him? Many anglers reach middle age without catching a trophy fish. Finally it was over. Eager African hands lifted the fish into the boat, and the dream had become reality. The dream however was not over yet, however. Within thirty minutes the boy had his second sailfish solidly hooked. I asked what he wanted to do with it. I expected him to take it in, for what boy can resist the brief glory of hanging his catch up in front of many spectators. I was wrong. 'Tag and release it,' he said. A brave decision for a small boy. Two hours later he caught a third sailfish. This one, too, was tagged and released. That day the boy had caught three sailfish. More importantly his personal doubts were answered. He could do it. He was a big game angler at last. The path from minnows to monsters had been paved with the sort of dreams that only a child can have. Those dreams had become reality.

INDEX